Praise for *Not Afraid*

"Bolelli is a genius warrior philo[...]
is the opposite of a victim's me[...]
ally apocalyptic experiences he h[...]
to anyone who is struggling with [...]
Everyone please listen, open your ea[...], and open your hearts to the
incredible, the brilliant, and the super sweet Daniele Bolelli."

—Duncan Trussell, comedian and host
of *The Duncan Trussell Family Hour*

"*Not Afraid* is an adventure story of the truest, deepest sort. In
recounting his story with enormous courage, sincerity, and wit,
Daniele Bolelli reminds us that real adventure *always* involves
great risk and, often, unimaginable loss. Life's toughest adventures
aren't the mountains we set out to climb or the jungles we explore;
they're the quiet challenges that come looking for us where we live.
You've never read a story like this or known a man like this. I rec-
ommend both without hesitation."

—Chris Ryan, *New York Times* bestselling author of *Sex at Dawn*

"An inspiring life story about overcoming fear. This is a necessary
task, no matter what you do in life. Whether you are an amateur or
professional athlete, you will be able to draw many similarities to
your sport. At the same time, this book gives us a great reminder to
enjoy the ride while it lasts. Well done, Daniele, you did it again!"

—Boštjan Nachbar, professional basketball player

"A true warrior poet, Daniele bleeds on these pages with fearless vulnerability and uncensored humor. The narrative starts with the challenges of a 'sensitive little nerd' overcoming his fear to turn pro in the
realest combat sport in the world, building momentum as it carries
the reader through his epic struggle with the death of his true love."

—Aubrey Marcus, writer and CEO of *Onnit.com*

"The honesty and authenticity in Daniele's writing is truly inspirational. Most books about life are written with kid gloves and give us old-school clichés to handle adversity. He gives us an honest look into the pain, heartache, and process of fighting back against things that would bring most to their knees. Everyone can relate to the feelings and thoughts Daniele displays. We can only hope to someday have his strength and conviction to come through and thrive!"

—AJ Hawk, 2011 Super Bowl champion with the Green Bay Packers

Praise for *Create Your Own Religion*

"With a cheerful, good-natured smile, Daniele Bolelli torpedoes the often luxurious but spiritually leaky battleships that sailed under the various flags of the world's organized religions."

—Tom Robbins, author of *Fierce Invalids Home from Hot Climates, Jitterbug Perfume, Still Life with Woodpecker*, and several other books

"The perfect cure to liberate our minds."

—Mike Vallely, professional skateboarder and wrestler, stuntman, and actor

"*Create Your Own Religion* challenges the pitfalls of blind faith."

—Ben Harper, Grammy award–winning singer-songwriter and multi-instrumentalist

"Daniele Bolelli is in the house. Minds will be blown. Lives will be changed."

—Joe Rogan, host of *The Joe Rogan Experience* and *Fear Factor*, UFC commentator

"Daniele Bolelli's book is a joy to read. It is clearly written and engaging, filled with humor and thought-provoking ideas. The questions he raises and the dialogue he creates is not only worthwhile but, I believe, essential."

—Shannon Lee, Bruce Lee's daughter and CEO of Bruce Lee Enterprises

NOT AFRAID

ON FEAR, HEARTBREAK, RAISING A BABY GIRL, AND CAGE FIGHTING

DANIELE BOLELLI

Published by Disinformation Books,
an imprint of Red Wheel/Weiser, LLC
with offices at:
65 Parker Street, Suite 7
Newburyport, MA 01950
www.redwheelweiser.com

ISBN: 978-1-938875-13-7

Library of Congress Cataloging-in-Publication data available upon
request.

Interior and text design by Frame25 Productions
Cover images: heart ©Chuhail/Shutterstock; baby carriage ©Janis
Abolins/Shutterstock; black belt ©Cristouao/Shutterstock

Printed in the United States of America
MG

10 9 8 7 6 5 4 3 2 1

For Isabella

*Of all that is written, I love only what a
person has written with his blood.*
—Friedrich Nietzsche

*Long as you're not afraid, nobody can run your life for
you. Remember that. Hell is being scared of things.
Heaven is refusing to be scared. I mean that literally. . . .
Now you know my religion.*
—Tom Robbins

Contents

Preface   xiii

Part I: Sparring with Fear

1. Why I Didn't Take the Blue Pill   3

2. *Tomoe Nage*, Misguided Telepathy, and Broken Ribs   8

3. Talk Less, Sweat More   13

4. A Cross Between Eminem and the Dalai Lama   17

5. I Had a Dream (Sorry, MLK!)   20

6. Joseph Campbell in the Cage   22

7. Where Illusions Go to Die   26

8. Zen Waves, the Wisdom of Drunkenness,
   and the Horrible Discovery That
   Inside My Mind Lives a Gnome
   Who Enjoys Screwing up My Life   30

9. My Stupid Ego, Buddhism, and the Roots of Fear   34

10. Sun Tzu and the Evil Russian
    (Latvian, Actually, But No
    One Knows Where Latvia Is)   37

11. "Scare the Shit Out of You" Is
    Not Just a Figure of Speech   41

12. I Should Have Stayed Home
    and Hugged My Teddy Bear   44

13. Fight Until Your Heart Explodes.
    And Then Fight Some More   47

14. Weight Training for Heart and Mind   54

15. The Drunken Taoist and the Power of Weirdness   57

16. The Wildly Inappropriate Sayings of Leo Hirai   63

17. Breaking a Good Man's Nose,
Cavan Cox and the Advantage
of Being Insane, and Other Tales   65

18. Courage and Love   70

19. Hoka Hey   75

Part II: Life and Death of a Wonderful Human Being

20. How an Incredibly Stinky Man
Inspired the Woman of My Dreams
to Talk to Me for the First Time   83

21. Bruce Lee Taught Me
That Love Trumps Stupid Rules   87

22. From the Pits of Hell   92

23. Doing Tai Chi Outside of a
Restaurant in Westwood after Midnight   99

24. How *Army of Darkness* Saved My Wedding   101

25. A Tiger out of the Cage   105

26. Nietzsche Would Have Been
Intimidated by Such Willpower   111

27. Giving Birth to a Baby in the Living Room   115

28. Heaven and Hell   121

29. The Moments That Can Crush Your Soul   124

30. "We Are Born into a World
in which no Quarter Is Given"   132

31. The Death of a Queen   140

32. The Smile   154

Part III: Answering Hopelessness with a Defiant Smile and Raised Middle Finger

33. "Throw Me into Hell, and
    I'll Find a Way to Enjoy It"   159

34. How Do You Tell a Nineteen-Month-Old
    Baby That She'll Never See Her Mother Again?   162

35. A Coldhearted Son of a Bitch   165
    Isabella Interlude 1: Isabella and Buddhism   169

36. Writing a Funny, Lighthearted
    Book While Dangling over the Abyss   171
    Isabella Interlude 2: Kate Upton   174

37. Fist, Please Let Me Introduce
    You to Wall. Wall, This Is Fist   176
    Isabella Interlude 3: Iz Is My Hero   181

38. Sipping Champagne among the Ruins   183
    Isabella Interlude 4: Empathy   186

39. Eminem, Medical Marijuana, and Trading
    Punches with Students . . . The Mystery
    of Why Academics Don't Like Me   188
    Isabella Interlude 5: Lullaby   191

40. Tupac and the Open Letter to Academia   192
    Isabella Interlude 6: Another Day at the Office   195

41. Answering Hopelessness with a
    Defiant Smile and Raised Middle Finger   196
    Isabella Interlude 7: Bad Words   200

42. "He Who Has Learned How to Die
    Has Learned How Not to Be a Slave"   202
    Isabella Interlude 8: The Next Jimi Hendrix   207

43. Truly Badass Is Having the
    Strength to Be Kind When Life Is Not   210
    Isabella Interlude 9: Clear Plans for the Future   213

44. Commencement Speech, Bolelli Style   214
   Isabella Interlude 10: Mulan and Being Like Other Girls   216

45. No Thoughts, No Swimming Trunks   217
   Isabella Interlude 11: Dog Costume   220

46. Don't Throw Away the Hero in Your Soul   221
   Isabella Interlude 12: A Four-Year-Old Dose of Reality 225

47. Goddesses of Mercy   226
   Isabella Interlude 13: Orlando Furioso   233

48. Tequila Pull-Ups   234
   Isabella Interlude 14: Mama Dreams   238

49. The Most Glorious Sixty-Two
   Seconds in the History of Moviemaking   239
   Isabella Interlude 15: Yakuza Style   243

50. PTSD   244
   Isabella Interlude 16: The Hobbit   248

51. The Podfather   249
   Isabella Interlude 17: Kids and Nightmares   253

52. How I Met Duncan Trussell and
   How a Drink Served in a London
   Bar Ended Up Being Named after Us   255
   Isabella Interlude 18: Facing Fear with Pink Band-Aids 258

53. The Drunken Taoist   260
   Isabella Interlude 19: Cannibalism   264

54. In the Beginning Was Fear   265

Acknowledgments   269

Preface

Hell showed up in my life unannounced. No warnings. No sense of impending doom. No bursting through the door screaming, "I have arrived!" My hell favored a subtle approach. It was a ninja who entered my house without being seen. It all began in such an unremarkable way that it barely registered as anything meaningful. Little did I know that the experiences of the next five months would rip me apart and kill me. They would also reforge me into a different man. Nothing was ever going to be the same again.

On that day, I became an unwilling traveler on a journey through the heart of fear. This book is the account of that journey. Every step along that path has forced me to face my fears time and time again.

Numerous people have pushed me to write about this. For a long time, I didn't see the point. A memoir? The thought made me want to throw up. It smacked of inflated ego, exaggerated sense of self-importance, and plain vanity. I was sure you'd have better things to do than to worry about the details of my life. Everyone has a story. And everyone runs into tragedy sooner or later. I didn't see anything unique in my own tale.

For a while, I thought about writing a philosophical dissertation about fear—something more universal and less personal.

But as Friedrich Nietzsche suggests in the opening quote, philosophy doesn't amount to much unless it comes straight from one's veins. If philosophy is not written with one's blood, then it's just idle chatter—useless noise. And nothing induces a writer to spill his guts on the page as much as addressing his own personal experience.

In the course of multiple podcast appearances, I noticed that whenever I spoke about ideas, people politely paid attention and may have been interested. But whenever I spoke about personal experiences, people were touched in ways I had never anticipated. Over time, I've received countless emails from individuals struggling with a myriad of terrible things in their lives—from dying relatives to their own dire health conditions, from lost jobs to heartbreaks, from fighting addictions to heavy depressions. And each time, they'd tell me how hearing about my own struggles encouraged them during desperate times. I still didn't really see why that was, but the fact that I was clearly too stupid to understand it was no reason to stop doing something that seemed to help people. And so, in this book, personal experience it is.

Inevitably, an emphasis on personal experience implies that some readers will find the specific examples resonating in their own experience while others may not. One doesn't need to share my exact same fears to find parallels in one's own life. It doesn't matter whether the main fear holding us back is the fear of death, the fear of how other people will judge us, the fear of rejection, the fear of giving your all but not being quite good enough, or any of the million other fears regularly seizing the hearts of most human beings. The process of facing one's fears is the same regardless of the specific example.

The story of my own sparring match with fear is divided into three parts: in the first I play with facing fear through fighting and martial arts. The second is the story of when Hell pays me a visit, and the death of my wife. The third is the story of raising my baby daughter after her mom's death and what happens in my life when my addiction to fear lessens.

Maybe someone may question what the martial arts section has to do with the rest of the book about my wife, my daughter, and the effects of what happened in my life. But the martial arts section has everything to do with what happens in the rest of the story. Dealing with fear through martial arts gave me the emotional muscles to face what I had to face. Without them, it would have been a very different story. Most of the themes that I had to deal with in real life showed up on the mat and in the ring first. Being exposed to increasing levels of stress in practice certainly helped me.

I have talked enough. Without further ado, let's go play.

PART I

Sparring with Fear

CHAPTER 1

Why I Didn't Take the Blue Pill

Fighting always scared the hell out of me.

And that's exactly why I have spent a good chunk of my life doing it.

Often, when people who know about my training and fighting in martial arts meet me, they look confused. I am nothing like what they expected. They had pictured encountering a killing machine with a mean streak and muscles growing even out of his ears, and instead they get my mellow, nerdy, glasses-wearing self. Their surprise is the same even if they don't meet me in person, and instead just talk to me on the phone. I don't exactly have a small, whiny voice, but I still don't exude that aggressive machismo—that gruff, grizzly-bear-who-just-woke-up-in-a-bad-mood vibe they had imagined.

I am freakishly sensitive, very emotional, nonconfrontational—a happy puppy who wants nothing but peace and love. I have spent thousands of hours with my head buried in books, and I hate conflict—physical or otherwise. So, it makes perfect sense that I would get into cage fighting, right?

If by now you are convinced that I must have flunked Logic 101 and I could use a refresher course, please indulge me and stay with me for the next few paragraphs as I make my case.

Ever since I can remember, I have always felt that it is the responsibility of any self-respecting human being to become a hero. By "hero" I don't mean the flashy, action movie stereotype of what a hero is supposed to be. What I am talking about is someone able to exude grace under pressure, someone capable of moving mountains if that's what it takes to bring a smile to those close to him, someone who doesn't let the deadly duo of weakness and laziness keep her from becoming the best person she can possibly be, someone who can take a beating at the hands of his inner demons and yet keeps getting back up, somebody with large metaphorical shoulders and a larger (equally metaphorical) heart. Since I was a kid, I felt that it was my duty (and everyone else's for that matter) to do this. Why should anyone settle for less?

But good intentions, clearly, are not enough. When everything is going well, under optimal conditions, it is not that difficult to be on your best behavior. The tricky part comes in when you find yourself under unbearable emotional pressure, when your body and your mind just can't take it anymore, and yet Life doesn't cut you any slack just because you are having a bad day. That's what heroism is all about—being able to embody your best even on the day when Life decides to deliver a Godzilla-sized kick to your groin.

This is why, when I would watch basketball as a kid, I wasn't as interested in players who could outscore everyone as I was in those who had the nerves of steel to sink the last shot when the game was on the line. A high shooting percentage is just a technical skill that isn't relevant outside the basketball court. Wanting the responsibility for the play that will decide the destiny of the game, and having the ability to rise to the moment even if—until that second—you may have had a horrible day, transcends technique: it's about possessing a mental and spiritual strength that is bigger than the game of basketball.

But yet my own experience has often fallen miserably short of my desires. Not infrequently, fear has found a way to spoil my heroic aspirations. My choice, then, was (and still is) obvious: I can give in to the shame of failing to live up to my ideals by ignoring it, so as not to be reminded of it on a regular basis. Or I can keep diving into those very experiences where Fear is most likely to be waiting to greet me.

Here is where fighting enters the picture. Few activities, in fact, force you to face your fears like fighting against someone determined to remove your head from the rest of your body.

I am not referring to an unexpected fight—when everything happens suddenly, and you find yourself too pumped with adrenaline to even have a chance to be afraid. I am talking about those fights that you know are coming, and you have plenty of time to anticipate and think about what is going to happen.

Many people consider the prospect of public speaking terrifying. But in public speaking all you have to worry about is yourself. In fighting, in addition to worrying about how you will play your part, you also have to worry about the unpleasant detail of that burly guy trying to break your bones and separate you from your consciousness. It's not enough to recite decently the speech you have gone over a million times, or perform a choreographed routine. Nothing is scripted here. You may have a general strategy, but you have to adapt it, and be ready to change it in a millisecond in order to respond adequately to what your opponent is doing. The stakes are higher than in most sports, where making a mistake leads to your opponent scoring a point. Here you don't just lose a contest and take a blow to your ego. In a fight, any mistake may lead to you finding your nose smeared across your face, and your bones waving at you after poking through your skin at very wrong angles.

In daily life, Fear is a ninja who can hurt us without ever showing its face. Without a crisis forcing it into the light of our consciousness, Fear does the most damage while hidden deep within us. It makes us too timid to take those very chances that excite us to the core. It convinces us to obey all the rules. It inhibits our willingness to question the way things are. It builds a cage around us. It turns our self-esteem into a bonsai—the necessary prerequisite for transforming us into dogma-craving followers of some authority figure. It shrinks our capacity to love and feel those emotions that shake our souls. It robs Life of its intensity, and makes us die long before it is time for us to check out.

And like a true ninja, it accomplishes all this undetected—without us even knowing it. So, it's possible to go through our time on this ball floating in space without realizing that Fear has been pulling our strings all along. Our inner tyrant has made for us most of our choices—even those we were not aware of making. The fucked-up part about it is that Fear makes it easy for us to go along with this. It doesn't hurt us in an obvious way. It numbs us before injecting us with its poison—a slow form of euthanasia that takes a few decades to come to its conclusion.

In combat, however, Fear quits pretending, and comes charging forward with a terrifying roar. It is dramatic. It is intense. And it makes no mystery that it's trying to crush your spirit.

In many ways, combat is truth. It is life lived after removing the veil of illusions that's usually wrapped around it. In the ring, in the cage, or on the mat, there's no place to hide.

It's one of the most uncomfortable, ugly feelings in the universe. It's like going on a date with pain, terror, and your own fear of death. It just makes you want to run away as quickly as possible in the opposite direction—definitely not a fun way to spend the day.

Early in life I managed to defeat my initial fears of public speaking in relatively quick and painless fashion. And I have been able to squash fear in several other fields. But when it comes to fear of conflict in general and physical violence in particular . . . well, that's a different story.

As much as dedicating myself exclusively to those fields where I naturally excelled would have been easy and probably more fun, it would have also been a cop-out—just another way to bury my head in the sand. And so I resisted the lure of the blue pill. For me, fighting was to be the place that would make me or break me. For better or worse, it was to be the place where I'd forge my spirit.

CHAPTER 2

Tomoe Nage, Misguided Telepathy, and Broken Ribs

This is my first memory of blind terror going hand in hand with martial arts.

In a large room in an elementary school in Milan, my hometown, I am standing in line with several other eight- and nine-year-olds. We are all scared shitless and incapable of opposing any resistance. We are like cows waiting for their turn at the slaughterhouse—with a vague premonition that something ugly is about to happen, but too frozen with fear to make a break for it.

This moment of pure panic comes to us courtesy of Mr. Evil himself, the little shit who just transferred into my school joining my third grade class. Up until this moment, going to school could occasionally be a rough business since I was always younger and smaller than everyone else in my classes, but in hindsight it had been nothing but a mellow warm-up for what awaited me. Once Mr. Evil showed up, I was about to be introduced to a whole new level of abuse.

He was a good-looking, seemingly ultra-confident son of a bitch, who immediately began initiating every other girl in the art of making out—a true nine-year-old player. Needless to say, it took me about seventeen seconds to begin hating him. He dominated in just about every sport he played. He was insanely popular. And he was the worst of tyrants. All of this was spiced up by the fact that he was more than a bit mentally deranged.

Here's a taste for you: on a weekly basis, his psychotic, attention-grabbing tendencies kicked into an extra gear and he'd begin screaming about killing himself by jumping out of the window. *Good riddance,* you say. Right? Not that simple as it turns out. If I didn't try to stop him, then he'd beat me up for not caring. And if I did . . . well, then he'd beat me up for stopping him. To add a cherry on this cake of ultimate mind-fucking, he had decided to befriend me. So, one second he'd be my trusted buddy and the next he'd try to kill me . . . about ten times a day. Being his friend was like riding on a schizophrenic tiger.

In any case, back to our dreaded room. As it turns out, the couple that had spawned Mr. Evil had the brilliant idea of enrolling him in judo classes. And Mr. Evil was anxious to turn everyone at school into guinea pigs for his martial experiments. On this day, he had convinced eight of us to line up and serve as test dummies for being thrown across the room. The fact that we had all sheepishly obeyed speaks volumes about the degree of control that he had on us.

At this time I didn't know a thing about judo, about its creator Jigoro Kano or his brilliant philosophy. All I knew was that it looked like it hurt.

A lot.

He tried the technique he had just learned the day before several times, but some technical detail was off, and one by one his guinea pigs were left off the hook with no damage.

And then it was my turn.

The little bastard grabbed me and hit the perfect *tomoe nage* technique. Lucky me! His foot on my stomach projected me to sail across the room for a surreally long time—only to crash against the door and collapse on the tiles without the benefit of a *tatami* to soften my fall. I was so happy I wasn't dead that I limped back to my feet and actually complimented him on his throw. Shit . . . they should have named the Stockholm Syndrome after me.

Inside my head, it was a different story. Besides giving myself about a 20 percent chance of finishing elementary school alive, all I could think was: *Fuck you Jigoro Kano, and fuck you judo for giving this little perverted sociopath the tools to torture us more effectively.*

Milan is a big city but somehow Mr. Evil's path trailed my own so that he ended up in the same schools as me until we graduated from high school (save for a temporary reprieve in junior high). Again, lucky me.

The dynamics never changed much. On one hand, he truly was my friend. When I was eleven years old, and I first began experimenting with writing, Mr. Evil would spend hours on the phone with me listening to every syllable I had committed to paper as if it were the best thing he had ever heard. He seemed to truly delight in listening to my stuff and never failed to give me extremely useful feedback. Having the enthusiastic support and encouragement of the most popular kid I had ever met did wonders for my confidence as a writer. For this, I'll always be in his debt. But then, of course, this didn't prevent him from dishing out abuse on a fairly regular basis.

Stupid me, I actually saved his ass once during the most misguided case of telepathy ever. We were eighteen and we had taken a trip with two lovely young ladies to a cabin in the mountains. (Luckily, I had not seen the *Evil Dead* movies yet!) On the second day, we all went for a very steep hike. I stopped halfway up the mountain to enjoy the view in the company of one of the girls. Being the competitive little prick that he was, Mr. Evil made a point to keep aiming for the top of the mountain, so he kept on. Girl #2 followed him. A couple of hours later, Girl #2 returned and we made our way back to the cabin. It was mid-afternoon. The logical thing to do would have been to bask in the undivided attention of both of those lasses, and make the best of it. Instead, after a while, I began to feel uneasy. I kept having this very strong, nagging feeling that something was wrong. Objectively, nothing was wrong. It was still early and the way up the mountain was long, so there was no reason to think anything bad had happened. But as much as I tried chasing this feeling away, it kept growing in intensity.

Oh, screw you, Mr. Evil! Spoiling my time with hot women even when you are not here? More than a bit annoyed and for no logical reason, I walked out and retraced my steps up the mountain. The girls looked at me with an expression that said "your loss." Damn . . . I still want to punch myself when I think about it. To make matters worse, there was no way I was going to run into him. The top of the mountain could be approached by literally a dozen different trails and I had no way of knowing which one was the correct one. I shrugged my shoulders, took a chance, and walked on. A couple of miles later, I heard the voice of Mr. Evil yelling for help. There was more than a hint of fear in his tone, so I quickened my pace. Not much later I ran into Mr. Evil himself—completely dehydrated, barely able to stand, and in full panic mode. The lack of food and water combined with a bit of heatstroke had royally kicked his ass. He had just sat down, unable to move another step. When he saw me, he was incredulous and overjoyed. Later he told me that he knew he'd never be able to make it back down the mountain alone, and had begun "calling" to me just about exactly at the time when I felt that uneasiness creep in. He couldn't believe I had found him. I couldn't believe I hadn't decided to finish him off right then and there when I had the chance . . .

After enduring years of his crap and even saving his sorry ass, I guess I was entitled to a taste of revenge. And my time eventually arrived. I had been training in martial arts for a couple of years. By now I was nineteen and living in the United States. I was back in Italy for a camping trip with many of my friends. Mr. Evil was there. In his usual effort to show off his macho supremacy, he had taken off his shirt to display his muscles and asked several people to hit him anywhere on his upper body—as if to say "I'm such a man that none of you little boys can do a thing to me." I gladly took the bait. As I got ready to hit him, I remembered how my martial arts instructors told me to always aim several inches behind my target for a more powerful blow. And so I did—breaking his ribs.

Oddly enough, we are still friends to this day. This, however, doesn't prevent me from dreaming every so often of meeting him in a cage fight and beating the living shit out of him. Some people say I should thank him, since it was his stupid *tomoe nage* and random abuse that pushed me on the path of martial arts, but I have watched the 1982 version of *Conan the Barbarian* too many times. When at the end of the movie, Conan's archenemy tells him that he should be thankful to him for giving him the incentive to become what he has become, Conan pauses for a second to ponder . . . and then he chops his head off.

CHAPTER 3

Talk Less, Sweat More

Looking back now, I can only smile remembering my initial approach to martial arts. Too many hours spent watching reruns of the *Kung Fu* TV series had skewed my perceptions a bit. I was hopelessly addicted to a romanticized image made of philosophically deep Zen sayings and aesthetically beautiful movements. I expected some wise old master—a cross between Yoda from *Star Wars* and Mr. Miyagi from *Karate Kid*—to take me under his wing and enlighten me about the secrets of the universe while levitating above the clouds in a lotus pose. Accordingly, my first few years of training were spent chasing this ghost. "Wax on, wax off, Daniel-san!"

Eventually, I began gravitating toward arts that traded pretty looks for a mean approach to self-defense. In particular, I stumbled upon a system known as Tsoi Li Ho Fut Hung (or more commonly, albeit less appropriately, as San Soo). Whereas most forms of kung fu taught today have rightfully earned a bad rep for being highly unrealistic and having lost whatever combat effectiveness they may have possessed in some distant past, San Soo seemed different. It lacked the flowery, stylish beauty of typical kung fu forms, and instead concentrated on your kick-their-groin, gouge-their-eyes type of stuff.

My focus had clearly changed. I was beginning to sense that, paradoxically, the road to the deep philosophical benefits of martial arts didn't pass through parroting fortune cookies, but through the seemingly rougher aspects of practice such as combat effectiveness and harder contact.

But even now that my purpose and direction were becoming clearer, my martial journey was complicated by a very pesky fact: every martial art is but a distant approximation of real combat. For safety reasons, they all try to simulate the experience of a real fight but with some limitations in order to allow you to go home in one piece. Most schools of martial arts follow either one of two approaches: they either train the full range of combat techniques—including those that for safety reasons are banned in sports—with a cooperative partner, or they limit the technical repertoire but train these fewer techniques with full speed and power against a resisting opponent. The first approach is privileged by schools specializing in self-defense, whereas the second is typical of martial sports. Clearly, each comes with its set of strengths and weaknesses. Self-defense arts employ the very techniques that one is most likely to use in a real life-or-death fight—the most effective, debilitating attacks possible. But the cooperative nature of their training results in lack of experience with timing, distance, adrenaline, and resistance. Martial sports do the exact opposite.

Training for many years in San Soo did wonders for my self-confidence, taught me some very valuable skills, and led me to meeting my wife. And yet, it didn't take long for me to grow restless. The training halls of most traditional self-defense arts (San Soo included) were crowded with too many talkers—too many people who are overeager to talk your ears off telling you how deadly and scary they really are. Hell . . . some of these guys spent more time inflating their egos through incessant talking than they did actually training.

It took me a while to figure out the reason for all this posturing. It all boiled down to the fact that cooperative training never gave them the feedback they needed. Without timing, sense of distance, adrenaline, ability to adjust to an overwhelming level of aggression being directed your way, and—most importantly—objective, measurable results, these practitioners never knew if their techniques would really work for them under pressure. Lacking concrete evidence reassuring them of their skill, they would end up convincing themselves by talking about what they *would do* in a real fight. In the process, they built such monumental egos that they ended up with too much at stake to actually test their theories. Their approach would become indistinguishable from that of religious fundamentalists: "it works because I say it does." It's Psychology 101, really . . . making a big show of confidence and certainties is actually the perfect indicator of someone being pathologically insecure.

The people who instead benefit the most by training cooperatively are those who have been in plenty of real fights. Like Jimmy H. Woo, for example, San Soo's top dog in America. According to all accounts of people who knew him, Woo was a very nice guy, but he came from a rougher time and place. So, let's just say that growing up he was on a first name basis with extreme violence. For someone like him, then, cooperative training was just a way to reinforce the lessons already tested through the fire of real combat. But for anyone who didn't share his familiarity with regular, bloody, life-or-death struggles, it wouldn't be enough. I was definitely in this latter category. For me, the biggest problem was that cooperative training didn't allow me to face fear in a real enough way. I just wasn't scared when I stepped on the mat. But to reap the best that martial arts had to offer, I needed to be.

This is why I eventually transitioned to combat sports. What I loved most about them was the excitement that comes from actually testing your theories, rather than just talking them to death. I welcomed the immediate, unforgiving feedback telling me whether a technique worked or not. And I also appreciated the non-indifferent side benefit of putting one's ego on the line in the heat of competition. Objective results, in fact, made it much more difficult to get lost in fantasies about one's own "deadly" skills. The beauty of competing is that it lets you know exactly where you stand and forces you to realize that on any given day anyone can be beaten.

I had spent enough time with my head buried in books and being surrounded by words. The last things I needed from martial arts were more debates and verbal arguments. What I craved was to talk less and sweat more.

CHAPTER 4

A Cross Between Eminem and the Dalai Lama

Once I began training with people who seriously tried to choke me unconscious and punch my head into tomorrow, everything changed. Confronting myself on a regular basis with fear and other unpleasant emotions made something click inside of me. The change didn't affect just my approach to fighting, but my way of thinking as well.

Other people noticed it too. A professor of mine in graduate school had asked us to write a lengthy research paper about any topic of our choosing in American Indian history. I had already taken several classes with him and it's safe to say I wasn't among his favorite people ever. (The same thing is also safe to say about how most academics feel about me, but that's beside the point.) Not that he hated me or anything, but he looked at me as an annoying hippie who approached Native American cultures in an unduly romantic way. So he was a bit taken aback when I told him I was planning to write about Crow Creek, the site of a 14th-century massacre in which one Native American group proceeded to murder, scalp, burn, dismember, and feed to the dogs members of another tribe—not exactly the kind of topic that suits the taste of people who spend their Saturday nights watching *Dances with Wolves* with starry eyes.

"What happened to you?" he asked me. "You seem different . . . did you change your perspective after reading those texts I suggested to you?"

"Not exactly," I replied. "I didn't read a word of them, but I did spend the last few months wrestling, doing jiu jitsu and MMA."

Perhaps I should have explained myself a tiny bit more. The question mark in his eyes told me he had no clue what the hell I was talking about. Perhaps the connection between picking up Mixed Martial Arts (MMA) and changing how I wrote about American Indian history wasn't quite self-evident. But since I like you more than I liked him, I'll make the effort and explain.

Combat sports put me on a diet of brutal pragmatism. They fed me a dose of reality with a side dish of roughness. This made me allergic to anything that was overly idealized and disconnected from what's earthy. It's as if until that point I had been listening to The Beatles, and combat sports introduced me to Jimi Hendrix. Not that there was anything wrong with The Beatles and their mellow love songs, but once I was exposed to somebody who could play with his teeth and set his guitar on fire, I couldn't get enough. Combat sports were reshaping my personality with a new edge that I had always missed.

I didn't lose track of what initially had attracted me to martial arts (and for that matter to American Indian Studies as well). I wasn't becoming less idealistic, and I certainly was far away from embracing cynicism. But I had developed a taste for a more nuanced, complex, gritty approach to things—one that wasn't afraid to mix philosophical depth and aesthetic beauty with a healthy dose of barbarian passion. One without the other felt contrived, fake, and stereotypical. I wanted and needed both, and training in combat sports was filling the gaps for me in this regard.

This combination of delicate sensitivity and gruff intensity is precisely what later ended up becoming the trademark characteristic of my writing and lecturing style. In the words of one of my history students, Julio, the bard from South Central, a man you can always count on if you need someone to dish out pure ghetto poetry, "You are like a cross between Eminem and the Dalai Lama. You can be really nerdy, and all deep and shit, but you are also raw as hell. Eminem without the bitterness. A Dalai Lama you can get drunk with."

Part of the reason why he had decided to befriend me was precisely because I could kick his gangster ass. He liked my ideas but his upbringing led him to have no respect for guys who can only talk the talk. He had no use for nice guys who didn't know what it meant to have your head stomped in a fight. He could only relate to those who were familiar with the darker, edgier side of life. After he had his chance to come train in martial arts with me, punch me in the face and notice it didn't faze me, he was intrigued. Once I shook off his punch and proceeded to choke him out, he was ready to listen to anything I had to say.

The only philosophy he had ears for came from the lips of those who enjoyed raw intensity more than the staleness of dusty scholars or the goodie-goodie vibes of new agers. Come to think of it, the same was true for me.

CHAPTER 5

I Had a Dream (Sorry, MLK!)

Zombies, vampires, serial killers, my high school teachers . . . all sorts of scary freaks regularly broke uninvited into my dreams, spoiling what was supposed to be a good night of sleep. Ever since I was a kid, I have always had the most vivid, terrifying nightmares. The details changed, but the substance was the same: being chased by someone wanting to do very bad things to me. I could never run fast enough. I could never hit them hard enough. Horror would close in on me, and there was nothing I could do about it. My breathing would become shallow. My mouth would turn dry. My heart sounded like the drummer of a punk band. Cold sweat froze me and burned me at the same time. And Terror played cat-and-mouse with me until I would wake up in a panic.

Everything changed on a particular night, after I had been training in martial arts for a decent enough time. But how were martial arts going to help me when it was my own subconscious that was torturing me?

It was 3 AM and I was in the middle of my usual encounter with freakish demons having a blast as the guest stars of my nightmares. The one hunting me down finally caught up with me, tackled me, and ended up on top of me. When I was about ten seconds away from waking up screaming, something different happened. As he leaned toward me, I headbutted him, breaking his nose. This gave me the time to steal the knife he was about to carve me with, and slash him across his eyes.

And then I was awake.

For the first time since I was born, what began as a nightmare didn't end with me curled up in a fetal position, overdosing on fear. Demons were screaming my name, but I convinced them that coming after me was not going to be conducive to their health. It was the most empowering feeling ever. It was as if all the hours spent training in escaping from every possible hold had saturated my muscle memory and my subconscious, making it impossible for me to fall back into the role of the defenseless victim.

This is how—from one day to the next—my nightmares lost their grip on me. Never again would I have one of those nights like I used to during the first two decades of my life. Still, today, a few times a year, my inner demons decide to try their luck again. For a moment, they quicken my pulse and give me a shot of anxiety, but the outcome is always the same—they drown in an orgy of blood. And I wake up—slightly disturbed by the insane level of violence I just unleashed against my own personal predators, but at the same time pleased not to have been their victim.

CHAPTER 6

Joseph Campbell in the Cage

The thing that attracted me most to MMA as a spectator before I even actively took them up was their mythic quality. MMA fights seem to offer a never-ending supply of moments that would have made Joseph Campbell happy.

There are moments in which sports stop being simple entertainment and turn into a sacred ritual. These are the moments in which technique becomes secondary to the true essence of the game—in which competition is no longer about pure athleticism, but is transformed into a battle between a man's spirit and his weaknesses.

Think of Michael Jordan in game five of the 1997 NBA finals. Before the beginning of the game, doctors tell him in no uncertain terms that there isn't a chance in hell that he'll be able to play that evening. Jordan, in fact, is knocked flat by a heavy fever, throws up worse than the protagonist of *The Exorcist,* and doesn't even have the strength to sit up in bed. Demanding the impossible from his willpower, Jordan manages to get up and takes to the court. Despite looking like he is about to pass out at any moment, MJ uses up the last bit energy he has left and scores thirty-eight points—including the winning shot—before collapsing in the arms of a teammate at the end of the game. Anyone who has ever seen that game has been witness to something that's much greater than basketball. That is what epic mythology is all about—a monumental testament of heart and guts. That is Exhibit A of what Nietzsche calls the "will to power."

Anyone who witnesses such heroic actions cannot avoid being inspired. These are experiences that—at least for a little while—cleanse us from cynicism and apathy, and remind us of the person that we have always dreamed of becoming. They are dry wood to feed our inner fire.

The same thing is true about the greatest movies, songs, and books. For a few hours, they kidnap you away from your surroundings and enlarge your soul. They remind you of what life can feel like. They are alarm clocks for what Nietzsche calls "the hero hidden in your soul." They are a call to arms, inviting you to get off your ass, set fire to the mediocrity that's swallowing you, and create the best life you can possibly have.

If this is true for fiction, if the unscripted drama of sports can create this result, this feeling is even more tangible in the primordial arena of combat where the stakes are much higher. Fighters in combat sports, in fact, face fear in a more direct and pure way than it's possible to do in any other sport. They strip down to the bare minimum and—armed with nothing but muscles and heart—put their physical well-being on the line every time they compete. It's almost inevitable, then, that such a primordial sport can create the kind of epic pathos that would have made Homer smile.

Like Kazushi Sakuraba, for example. I can't think of any other fighter whose career better embodies the warrior mythology. Here's a man who, for well over a decade, made a habit of fighting opponents a couple of weight categories above his—and still managed to shine. Think of his match against Royce Gracie. The multiple time UFC champion had agreed to face Sakuraba only if the rules were modified to his liking: no time limits, no judges, and fifteen-minute rounds to continue until either one of them was knocked out or gave up. The referee wouldn't have the power to stop the fight. Sakuraba agreed to fight under these rules, which seemed to have been taken straight from *Rollerball*, and thus began the longest match in the modern history of MMA. After ninety minutes of fighting (yes, you read right, ninety minutes!), Gracie couldn't stand any more, and his cornerman was forced to throw in the towel.

But what turned Sakuraba into a god of the martial arts happened later on that same night. The match against Royce, in fact, was the quarterfinal of a tournament that would continue on that very day. Despite the ninety-minute battle that had just ended, Sakuraba returned to the ring shortly afterward for his semifinal match. His opponent was Igor Vovchanchyn, one of the most feared strikers in the world at that time, and a heavyweight who outweighed Sakuraba by about forty pounds. After another fifteen minutes of very even fighting, the judges ordered a supplementary round to break the draw. Only at this point did Sakuraba's corner finally decided to give him a rest and forfeit the match . . . this is the kind of tale that just hearing about it would be enough to drive Homeric heroes to hide under the blankets, hugging their teddy bears.

Nearly ten years later, despite his age and many injuries, Sakuraba could still pull off martial miracles. His 2009 match with Zelg Galešić is one of the most dramatic examples of willpower and resilience ever staged in MMA. As soon as the fight began, Saku took Galešić down with a single leg. The Croatian, however, defended well against Sakuraba's submission attempts, and even managed to hit him repeatedly as Saku was trying to work a leglock. In a scene that defies reason, Sakuraba didn't even flinch as Galešić hit him with fifty-nine consecutive punches. Saku survived this barrage and extended Galešić's leg, finishing him by kneebar. Who in the world can remain calm while being bashed with fifty-nine punches to the head—too busy trying to apply his own technique to pay attention?

And this is only one of many examples that Sakuraba's career offers. From his surreal resurrection against Smirnovas to the eerie calm with which he handled Quinton Jackson's fury before finishing him off, every minute that Sakuraba spent in the ring is a master class about what it means to be a warrior. And what's even more extraordinary is the fact that Sakuraba is not one of the macho, tough fighters who seem to have been born out of a rock, but is a very relaxed, mellow, gentle man who loves spending his time making people laugh.

CHAPTER 7

Where Illusions Go to Die

Five seconds into my first MMA fight, and I already had a right hand landing square in my face. This was not quite what I had expected.

It was just a smoker fight—one of those unofficial competitions set up in some gym in front of no more than a hundred people or so. And the rules were painfully stupid: no striking on the ground and only fifteen seconds of ground work before returning to the feet. Despite the silly rules, this was supposed to be easy for me, at least on paper. Too bad fights don't take place on paper.

By this time I had about a decade of experience in martial arts, and was a highly ranked black belt in San Soo, whereas my opponent had less than a year of training. I had a chance to spar with him a few times, and I beat him every time. But this was not a sparring session, and belts mean less than shit once punches begin to fly and the adrenaline begins to flow.

I came out of the gate looking to score with a low kick right away. Maybe it was the nerves of fighting in front of an audience, or maybe I hadn't switched out of sparring mode into fight mode, but I missed by a mile. He stepped out of the way and countered with a hard right. I had officially been welcomed to the world of fighting. The right hand was the first of several messages informing me that fighting against someone pumped with endorphins was an entirely different business from what I thought.

Among the annoying discoveries I made in the first minute was the fact that my takedowns—which had always looked cool in practice—had migrated to warmer climates and were nowhere to be found. So, when I realized that I was more comfortable fighting on the ground (oddly, the aspect of fighting in which I had, at that time, the least amount of training), I ended up shamelessly pulling guard several times. My opponent, on the other hand, racked up points by shooting a couple of very decent double legs. In the first round I had a few good moments. Early on, I caught him in a good Muay Thai clinch and landed some solid knees, quickly transitioning to a guillotine choke that looked tight, but the bastard didn't tap, and the ref stood us up. I could console myself by noticing how he had turned purple because of the choke, but it was hard to find consolation when the now-purple bastard didn't slow down, and instead kept rocking me with some insanely hard shots.

In between rounds, Fear came to pay me a visit. It was clear that things were not going the way I wanted, but I cut the visit with Fear short by formulating a plan. I knew exactly what combination I wanted to use as soon as the next round began. If I landed it correctly, he'd be taking a nap on the ground in no time.

Everything happened as if by magic. He took the bait of my initial feint and left himself open for my attack. I landed a hook that made his head spin. For good measure, I doubled up with a second, equally powerful punch. Based on everything I had been taught, he should have been out by now, and the fight should have been over. Instead, a fraction of a second later, far from collapsing into a heap, he shook it off and stepped forward to press a counterattack.

That's when I knew I had lost the fight.

I had hit him as hard as I could, and it hadn't even slowed him down?! Was I stuck in some horror flick in which the bad guy keeps coming after you no matter how many times you kill him? Didn't they teach this evil freak the laws of physics in school? Didn't he know that he was supposed to fall and stay down? Why wasn't he quitting?

Well . . . say hello to adrenaline, Mr. Bolelli.

I was paying the price for having trained for too long in traditional martial arts that didn't take into account the adrenaline factor. In the comfort of the training hall, fighting had looked so logical and orderly. All I had to do was worry about proper technique, and the rest would take care of itself. My teachers had said nothing about emotion and about the crazy things people were capable of when filled with adrenaline.

I mentally went over the names and faces of all of my martial arts teachers, and I hated them. I sincerely hated them all.

It was like a veil had been lifted, and I now saw fighting for the first time. It became perfectly clear that most of the black belts I knew would be completely lost in a real fight. Unlike what happened in Brazilian jiu jitsu (where you had to fight and win in order to advance in ranking), in many traditional arts belts were given for the time and effort you put into training and for performing set techniques during an exam. They were not based on any objective criteria that tested effectiveness. Some black belts I trained with were truly excellent, but most might as well have had a black belt in flower arranging, because their fighting skills were pathetic.

Finding out that I belonged to this latter category hurt more than all the punches I had been hit with.

The rest of the match went downhill from there. I got hit—a lot—before one last chance to finish the fight. Off my back, I caught him in a perfect armbar. I got to crank it quite a bit—more than enough to convince people to tap during training. But this was not training, and we had already established that my opponent was a sociopathic maniac who was impervious to pain and common sense. So, he didn't tap. And I was not savvy enough on the ground to use the armbar to sweep him, so he ended up stacking me and winning the match on points.

A little over two years later, I had a chance to rematch him in another smoker. An improved wrestling technique allowed me to take him down and hit him with a punch that packed all the frustration I felt during our first encounter. Before the first round was over, I finished him off with a heel hook.

Redemption had been achieved and I could be happy then, right?

No. I won the rematch because of some technical adjustments, not because I had defeated fear. As it turned out, this would be much harder than learning a couple of new techniques.

CHAPTER 8

Zen Waves, the Wisdom of Drunkenness, and the Horrible Discovery That Inside My Mind Lives a Gnome Who Enjoys Screwing up My Life

Being the weird, little nerd that I was, at eleven years old I read a book entitled *Zen Flesh, Zen Bones*. Out of the 101 Zen stories collected in the book, only four or five "clicked" for me (in case you are keeping tabs, after many more reads, I now "get" about forty). Among those that made perfect sense to me the first time around was one entitled "O-Nami"—which is both the name of the protagonist of the story and the Japanese terms for "great waves."

The plot revolved around a popular fighter from the Meiji era. His strength and technical skills were first-class, so that in private bouts he defeated even his own martial arts teachers. But being a big, fearsome fighter didn't spare him from being painfully shy. So, in public he'd regularly get trashed by low-level fighters. In order to find a solution to his dilemma, O-Nami visited a Zen teacher who prescribed him a cure for his mental hang-ups. Reminding him of his name, "Great Waves," the Zen teacher told him to stay in the temple all night to meditate on the power of the waves.

"You are no longer a wrestler who is afraid"—he said—"You are those huge waves sweeping everything before them . . . Do this and you will be the greatest wrestler in the land."

And so O-Nami complied. After some initial difficulties, he was able to focus on the feeling of the waves crushing everything in their path. As the story describes, "As the night advanced, the waves became larger and larger. They swept away the flowers in their vases. Even the Buddha in the shrine was inundated. Before dawn, the temple was nothing but the ebb and flow of an immense sea."

By the time the Zen master came back in the morning, he noticed O-Nami had a huge smile on his face. "Nothing can disturb you now," he told him. "You are those waves. You will sweep everything before you."

And the last line of the tale informs us that O-Nami dominated the competition that very day, and never lost another fight again.

What this story clearly underscores is how essential the mind is in a fight. Here you have a fighter who is technically as good as it gets, but who is also—in the immortal words of Tito Ortiz—"a mental midget." Technique and fighting spirit are entirely separate skills, and both are badly needed. One without the other only goes so far.

Taoist prankster Chuang Tzu makes a similar point in the following passage:

> In an archery contest, if the prize is a certificate, an archer will be relaxed and use all his skill. If the prize

is a silver trophy, he may become hesitant. When the prize is a golden statue, he might shoot as if he were blind. The archer's skill is the same in all three occasions, but in the two latter cases he's affected by his nerves and magnifies the importance of the prize. Attaching too much importance to external things makes you careless about internal ones.

By contrast, Chuang Tzu also notes that someone whose mind is relaxed can accomplish things that are impossible to those frozen with tension. In a classic example, which proves that drunk drivers predate cars, he mentions that when drunks fall from their carriages, they rarely get hurt as sober people do because their bodies are free from anxiety and rigidity.

Since being smashed out of your mind may make you relaxed but not exactly alert, it follows that the ideal frame of mind for fighting is a mix of two opposite qualities—a state of relaxed alertness, which, incidentally, is also the best frame of mind for most other endeavors in life as well.

Well . . . thanks Chuang Tzu. Thanks Mr. O-Nami. Your point is well taken. This is all sweet and all, but how exactly do you get to that state? Understanding it intellectually is a far cry from actually pulling it off. It's like telling someone suffering from insomnia that sleeping is very good for him. I tried to meditate on the fuckin' waves, but it didn't do it for me. I was still scared shitless. So, now what?

Thinking about this stuff, however, made me realize a horrible truth. I'm a bona fide black belt in psyching myself out. It's as if there was a damned gnome inside my mind who enjoys screwing up my life, by sabotaging me with fear and anxiety precisely when facing challenges that require me to be confident and at ease. I could train martial arts techniques from here to forever, and yet it wouldn't help me stop the laughing little gnome from doing his evil work. After this realization, much of my life both in and out of martial arts would be spent trying to figure out a way to lure the little bastard out of my mind (a pot of gold, perhaps? Or a hot, shapely gnome lady? Or whatever else these diminutive freaks are into . . .) so that I can beat him senseless. Let's see if you'll laugh then, tiny demon from hell. But as it turns out, the miniature nemesis is crafty, and it'll not be easy to catch him.

CHAPTER 9

My Stupid Ego, Buddhism, and the Roots of Fear

As scary as fighting is, it's also true that it's not that scary.

Try again, Bolelli? What the hell did you just say?

Full contact fighting is not war, where the chances of dying or of leaving some essential body parts on the battlefield are high. You can get hurt and injured—sure. But you are 99.9 percent guaranteed that you'll be home for dinner, and life will go on. So, why should anyone be so scared of fighting?

I have asked myself this question many times. Just the simple fact of facing something potentially unpleasant and painful doesn't seem to warrant the sheer terror that many people—me among them—feel at the prospect of fighting.

A clue to a possible answer showed up in my consciousness when I realized that I am not the least bit scared by grappling competitions. The thought of having to tap out from a choke, an armlock, or a leglock doesn't raise my blood pressure.

But at the same time, it's not like I am all that scared at the thought of getting hit either. I have been hit plenty of times, and it really isn't that bad.

So, why be afraid?

Deep down, the fear of fighting may have to do more with one's ego than with the fear of physical pain. Perhaps, what it really is all about is the fear of being physically dominated by another man, of being bullied, of being humiliated.

Getting outgrappled in martial arts, or outscored in most other sports, may be annoying, but it is not nearly as emasculating as having somebody sit on top of you and beat the shit out of you while you can't do anything about it.

Can this be it? Is my ego truly this big?

Apparently so—but maybe with good reason.

In one case, you are just losing a game. In another case, you are the victim in a primordial struggle for power. Losing a fight is less about being defeated in a sport, and more about evoking the ancestral memories of what it means to be crushed by your enemies when your own life and the lives of everything you love are at stake. If you let your enemies physically overpower you, they'll conquer your lands, chop your head off, use your skull as a drinking vessel at their victory party, rape your women, and piss on the altars of your gods. (I paint quite a picture when I get fired up, don't I?)

Even though clearly this is not what will happen if you lose an MMA fight, on a visceral level it can feel that way. The very raw, primordial nature of an all-out fight can trick the ego into feeling that more is at stake than it really is. Rightly or wrongly, for some people it feels like your very self-worth as a man is on the line.

The particularly messed-up thing about fighting is that the odds are excellent that what you fear will materialize. Not the rape-pillage-and-turning-your-skull-into-a-drinking-cup part. But it's almost guaranteed that at some point you will lose, quite likely in humiliating fashion. Even the very best fighters in the world are rarely immune to this. Think of Chuck Liddell, a man who dominated his weight class for several years, finishing his career with his arms flailing, his eyes rolled into the back of his head, falling unconscious, face-first on the canvas. Or think of Fedor Emelianenko, a fighter who had been widely considered the greatest example of invincibility in MMA, looking sadly helpless as he got beaten into a pulp by Antônio Silva. It almost doesn't matter how good you get. If you keep fighting long enough, you'll eventually run into someone who, on a given night, will be better or luckier than you, and who will brutally beat you and make off with your lunch money.

So the enemy that's going to paralyze you with fear is your own sense of self-importance and your excessive ego. The thought of not living up to the image of yourself that you want everyone to see is a source of tremendous anxiety.

At the end of the day, attachment is what kills you.

Buddhism holds that being attached to how you want reality to be will make you reap a harvest of unhappiness any time reality doesn't cater to your desires. This is not exactly a religious belief that requires faith as much as it is a fact of life. As the equation goes, the stronger the attachment is, the deeper the misery.

The trick about this is that the source of the problem finds its roots in our desires and our passion for life—things that clearly no one wants to get rid of, since they are precisely what make life fun.

What we are left with, then, is a paradox: being able to be passionate, emotional, and full of desire, and yet becoming so centered that our happiness is not wrapped around whether our wishes come true or not. Being able to have fun tasting life in all of its intensity, yet being relatively unaffected by the cards that reality decides to deal to us, is as useful for fighting as it is in every other aspect of life.

Needless to say, this is a lot fuckin' easier said than done.

CHAPTER 10

Sun Tzu and the Evil Russian (Latvian, Actually, But No One Knows Where Latvia Is)

Getting my ass kicked in my first MMA outing left me with two choices: decide that it wasn't for me and turn away, or go back to the drawing board. And so the drawing board it was.

My technique could use some serious improvement in both striking and grappling, so it was a matter of figuring out which holes in my game required the most immediate attention.

Boxing, Muay Thai, and other striking arts are obviously an essential part of the arsenal of anyone picking up MMA, but—even though I would eventually train in boxing for a few years—I seemed to be more naturally drawn to grappling.

Besides my own inclination, grappling training had some objective advantages. By relying on seeking victory through takedowns, chokes, and joint locks—which can be practiced relatively safely—they offer the chance to test the techniques with full speed and power against resisting opponents. Striking training is a little trickier since, if you spar too hard on a regular basis and take too many head shots, you can quickly kiss good-bye to some brain cells. And if you go too soft, you are not training realistically enough.

And so it was settled. I'd become a grappling convert.

For a while I played with judo. I just loved the aesthetic beauty of judo throws! But I ended up hating the fact that judo was overly dependent on the use of the *gi*—whereas in MMA there is no jacket you can grab to set up the throws.

Much uglier-looking, but also much more applicable, was training in wrestling: it was quite possibly the most important martial arts instruction I ever received, and it would completely change my way of fighting. The experience on the mat confirmed what I had already understood intellectually: a quick analysis of the MMA game told me that wrestling was the single most important piece of the puzzle. Even if you become the best striker in the world, it will not help you unless you have the defensive wrestling skills to keep the fight on the feet. And if you are a groundfighter, it doesn't matter how good you are on the ground if you don't have the takedowns to bring the fight there.

If I was going to make groundfighting my specialty, in addition to picking up some solid wrestling basics, I needed to intensify my study of Brazilian jiu jitsu, and I did.

But just as important as arming myself with these new tools was becoming skilled at crafting perfect game plans to minimize risks and exploit my opponent's weaknesses. As good, old Sun Tzu teaches in *The Art of War*, through a great strategy it's possible to win a fight before it even begins. Any self-respecting opponent will be better than you in at least some facets of the game, so the key to victory is in directing the fight away from his strengths.

I was reminded of this just a few days ago when, while grocery shopping, I ran into the Evil Russian (Latvian, actually, but no one knows where Latvia is, so we'll just pretend he was

Russian). For a second, I recognized his face but couldn't quite place him. He similarly seemed to recognize me but didn't say hi. He just looked at me, mumbled something in Russian (or was it Latvian?) and turned away. I was left wondering what I could have possibly done to deserve all this chilly hatred by this proud specimen of the former Soviet Union, and then it all came back to me... Our first meeting in a boxing ring a few years earlier flashed in my mind. On paper, our matchup had suicide written all over it. The bastard was taller than me, stronger than me, younger than me, faster than me, and had much better boxing technique. But, as it turned out, I beat his ass anyway. No wonder he hated me.

The demise of the Evil Russian (or Latvian, or whatever) boiled down entirely to strategy. Considering that he had every physical and technical advantage, it really didn't look like there was much for me to do other than find a place to get hit and fall down. But I was smarter than him, and I milked this for all I could. Since he was a head taller than me and kept a fairly straight stance, I crouched low, forcing him to throw punches at a very weird angle. At the same time, I countered by throwing strikes from the weirdest possible directions—ugly punches, but effective since they were so far from orthodox boxing techniques that they caught him by surprise. I also shot in on him almost wrestling-style so I could turn our match into a clinching brawl in order to nullify his speed. I used every dirty boxing trick in the book. I arm-dragged him, pinned his gloves to his body, stepped on his feet, hit him every time we broke the clinch, and a dozen other things that were illegal enough to be effective, but not so flagrant as to be called. By the end of the match, he looked dejected. He just couldn't understand how or why someone so clearly weaker and less skilled than him had beaten him during every round. Apparently, they didn't study Sun Tzu in Russia (or Latvia, or wherever the hell he had come from).

This would eventually become my greatest strength in MMA: my athletic skills were never more than average, but my understanding of the game was deeper than most, and this gave me the ability to come up with ideal strategies for every type of opponent.

Unfortunately, however, this was great if my only goal was to win fights, but it did nothing to help me defeat fear. And the same can be said for training in judo, Brazilian jiu jitsu, and wrestling: great technical fixes to the holes in my game, but not what I needed to address fear itself.

Not knowing what to do about conquering my fears, I figured that I had to step back on the mat to find out. In my next smoker, I faced off against a good judo player with very decent striking. I took all of five seconds from the beginning of the match before I put my wrestling to use, shot in, and took him down. I quickly transitioned to mount, threw a single punch in order to get a reaction, and put him in an armbar as soon as he raised his hands. My experience with my previous opponent not tapping led me to crank the armbar too hard and too fast. Luckily his arm didn't break, but I still felt horrible about my lack of self-control.

In the following match, I picked up another victory that was a carbon copy of the first. Since my approach seemed almost entirely grappling-based, it would have made sense to dedicate myself exclusively to submission grappling competitions, but A) I hated the rules and point system of submission grappling tournaments, and B) it would have been self-defeating. I wasn't scared of grappling, and the whole point of competing was coming to terms with fear, so MMA is where it would be for me.

Considering the results, it may have looked like things were changing for the best, but the only thing that had changed was better technique. Inside, I was as scared as always.

CHAPTER 11

"Scare the Shit Out of You" Is Not Just a Figure of Speech

It's 7 AM on fight day, and I'm already enjoying my fourth trip to the bathroom. Judging from past experience, this will not be the last. As I found out when I began competing in MMA, "scare the shit out of you" is not just a figure of speech. Besides giving you an impossibly dry mouth, a heavy sense of nausea, cold chills, shallow breathing, and horrendously stiff muscles, the physiology of fear has other gifts in store for you. Among other things, it delivers an immediate eviction notice to everything you have eaten in the last week, and doesn't let up until all illegal squatters have been kicked out of your stomach.

The great thing about fear is that it doesn't let you slide by lying to yourself. This is also the horrible thing about fear. You can fake not being afraid all you want, but all the physical symptoms make it impossible to lie. Every time I think that fear is a thing of the past, fight day arrives to let me know that all my wishful thinking just crashed face-first into reality.

In addition to bringing my consciousness to the unpleasant surprise that, despite my best efforts, I'm still a wimp, the morning bathroom ordeal has other negative side effects. Everyone cuts weight before the weigh-ins, and quickly gains it back by drinking and eating plenty. In this way, by the time they walk up to the cage, 99 percent of fighters are considerably heavier and stronger. For me, it's a different story. Thanks to the bathroom marathon, I am one of the very few people (I'm hoping I have company here but I'm not so sure) who weighs less by fight time than they did at the weigh-ins.

Every single time this happens, as I am sweating and struggling for a deep breath, I swear to myself that this will be the last time that I'll put myself through this. The evil gnome from a few chapters ago whispers in my ear, *You are not cut out for this. Other people may be able to handle the pressure. You obviously can't. So, make this the last time we do this.*

C'mon, you little freak, this is hard enough without your comments. Don't you have a pot of gold to look for or whatever else you jolly, bearded sons of bitches enjoy doing? Just get on with it and leave me alone.

Sometimes, the inner gnome takes it even further and reminds me that I can still pull out of the fight at the last minute (btw, I'll quit with the gnome thing for now since it's making me sound more schizophrenic than I mean to).

In reality, I'm not fooling anyone. Deep down, I know that I will not pull out of the fight, and I know that this will not be the last time. But giving myself a possible way out lessens the terror at least a little bit.

The way fear assaults the body is brutal, but the body has a few resources to fight back with. Certain physical actions can, at least temporarily, send fear packing. Once fear loosens its grip on the body, the mind will follow. Heat is one of the medicines

I have discovered in my experiments for regaining some sanity before a fight. I have no idea why, but warming up the body to the point of breaking out in a sweat quickly shrinks fear. And this is why I often blast the heater in my car driving up to a fight—even in summer. Cold—vice versa—seems to give fear an injection of steroids.

Another useful trick I picked up along the way is the yoga posture popularly known as "happy baby." Again I am clueless to the reasons why it works, but holding the posture brings a smile to my face, plus it enables me to distinctly feel fear leaving my body. This only lasts for a little while—fear is quick to regain its hold once I let go of this posture—but "happy baby" gives me a brief respite when I feel that I am about to crack.

CHAPTER 12

I Should Have Stayed Home and Hugged My Teddy Bear

This is—hands down—the lowest point of my martial arts career.

It is my sixth smoker fight, and in attendance is the biggest audience I have fought in front of so far. The worst part about it is that I know absolutely nothing about my opponent, and this has made it impossible to formulate a strategy. For a control freak like me, this is a hellish punishment. Not knowing . . . simply drives me crazy.

The bell rings and no more than three seconds later my opponent throws a kick aimed for my head. Reacting by instinct I immediately shoot in, but he sprawls very well, so I end up in my guard. He hits me with a particularly heavy punch, but I have a surprise waiting for him. I let him pass to half guard just so I can sweep him to end up in a perfect position to finish him with a leglock. I crank the Achilles lock and . . . for about fifteen seconds it looks like I have him and he is about to tap, but he manages to work through the pain and escape. We are barely over a minute into the fight and he has just passed to side control.

And this is where something I had never anticipated happens . . . I just tap out . . . Not because he has a submission technique on me. Not because he is hitting me. Not for any seemingly logical reason. I just tap.

I tap because I want out of there. I tap because now that my first plan hasn't panned out, my brain just gave up. I tap because I'm a wimp.

In the following minutes, I'll come up with several different plausible reasons why I tapped out, but the reality is that the only reason why I did it was because I was frozen stiff with fear and couldn't bring myself to fight through adversity. If there is such a thing as a warrior spirit, what I just displayed is the exact opposite of it.

A couple of days later, I am still too shell-shocked to come to terms with my minute in the ring. They say that in a fight you discover who you truly are. If that's the case, I really don't like the person I am. As Steven Pressfield wrote in his book *Gates of Fire*, "I had seen my own heart and it was the heart of a coward. I despised myself with a blistering, pitiless scorn."

On the phone, a friend tries to break the news to me. He was there. He saw what happened. And he believes he knows what's up: "You are simply not a fighter." He tells me. "You are an intellectual. You are good with words and shit. Fighters can't talk or write or lecture or think the way you do. So, you can't expect to be as tough as they are. You have plenty of talents, but they are not in fighting."

If this is supposed to console me, it fails miserably. Those words—that are meant to help me—hurt more than I have ever been hurt in the ring. And what is even worse is that I can't deny what he is saying. I mean . . . after what I have done, what could I possibly say to deny the obvious truth of his words? It's as if any pride I have ever felt in myself vanished in that second in which my hand tapped the mat.

In a sense, my friend is right. I am not a fighter. I am a sensitive little nerd. I cry at movies. And I am scared of my own shadow.

But he is also missing the damned point. I am trying to become more than I have been up until now. I don't want to accept my existing limitations as an immutable sentence, or some sort of inevitable destiny. I am tired of being afraid. I am tired of being intimidated by conflict. I am tired of shrinking in the face of hardship. And when a horde of demons will burst out of hell screaming my name, they will not be impressed with how well read I am, or with the fact that I am nice, sweet, and have good manners. The only thing that will matter is whether I can take everything they dish out and have any strength left to laugh in their face.

This is not just about fighting in the ring or excelling at some sport. If that was it, he'd be right: my energies would be better spent doing something else, since I clearly am not a natural at this game. But fighting for me is directly related to how I think and how I write. It is directly related to what type of husband, friend, and father I can be. This is about forging the heart and guts that I, and everyone I love, can depend on. This is about not always being a hostage of my own fear of death—and of life.

So, my dear friend, thanks for your concern, but fuck off.

CHAPTER 13

Fight Until Your Heart Explodes.
And Then Fight Some More

Less than a month later, the bell rings again and I am staring at a new guy wanting to punch my face into the ground. *Yes, finally!*

I have been waiting for this since within a few minutes after tapping out the last time. I needed to get back to fighting as quickly as possible, or I would have driven myself crazy thinking about my last shameful outing. I needed another match as much as I needed oxygen. And so I jumped at the first opportunity: an eight-man tournament—direct elimination style. My regular prefight ritual (sheer terror and bathroom marathon) has been spiced up by the fact that wildfires have been scorching the land close to my house, so I've had to spend the morning loading boxes and getting out of the way before the flames decide to BBQ my ass. In some odd sense, it's actually a good thing, since it prevents me from having too much spare energy to stress out.

The tournament is supposed to be reserved to 155-pound fighters, but somebody must not be very good at math, because my opponent is a good four inches taller and twenty-five pounds heavier than me . . . oh, joy! Since this is an unregulated event, the organizers have decided to dispense with details such as weigh-ins. I mean . . . we are not so old-fashioned as to believe in weight categories, are we? My opponent is a decent striker but his grappling skills are awful, which means that the strategy for this fight is quite obvious: stay out of range and move in only to shoot for a takedown.

Things unfold according to plan. I take him down and move on to a submission fairly quickly. I could swear I hear him yell out a verbal submission, so I let go of his arm, but the ref heard nothing of the sort and lets the match continue. I am furious, but there's nothing I can do about it, so I'm back to Plan A, and I take him down again. On the ground, his strength is giving me a harder time than expected. Plus, he does an excellent job at throwing strikes from the bottom to throw me off my game. It's only several minutes later, in the second round, that I manage to hit him with a power shot to the solar plexus that rewrites the rules of our interaction. He pretty much deflates to the point where you can almost see his fighting spirit leaving his body. This makes it easy for me to pass his guard, take top mount, and lock up an armbar. But I guess not all of his fighting spirit has gone on vacation yet, since he refuses to tap. This time I take no chances, so I inform him that he has two seconds to tap before I break his arm. Proving that his IQ is stronger than his fighting spirit, he wisely decides it's a good time to tap out.

Despite the win, all my friends are laughing their asses off at my expense: I'm the only idiot they know who in competition gives a warning to his opponent rather than just taking his arm home as a souvenir. Next time—they suggest—perhaps I should send him a letter pointing out the error of his ways, and politely requesting his cooperation in resolving the matter. Damn nerdy wimp . . .

In the meantime, our eight-man tournament has quickly downsized into a four-man tourney. Two winners are too injured to continue, so my semifinal match has just been upgraded to the final of the whole event. The only other winner who is healthy enough to fight again soon is a physical specimen named Leo Hirai. He doesn't weigh much more than I do, but the man has a six-pack even in his eyelids. In his first match, he dominated his opponent by sitting on top of him, wrapping one arm around his neck, and dropping punches until the ref rushed in to stop a textbook example of brutal "ground and pound."

My friends are not laughing so much anymore. From the look in their eyes, it's obvious they believe I am about to get killed.

Despite my wimpy tendencies, I am not quite as worried as they are. After all, I fought against Leo a few months earlier, so I know what to expect. Our first encounter ended without any submission or knockout. It was a good, hard-fought battle. I felt I was ahead on points but, since there were no judges, if I want to be fair I guess it'd have to be considered a draw. Or maybe not . . . it's my book and I don't feel like being fair, so I'll still put it in the win column. Hirai definitely disagrees with this but . . . well, fuck you, Leo, write your own damn book to argue your point.

In any case, the moral of the story is that I had fought him already, and I did quite decently, so I know he is not going to walk right through me like he did with his first opponent in the tournament. This, however, clearly doesn't prevent me from being scared out of my mind.

As we begin the first round, it's obvious that Leo is one of those very annoying fighters who perform in the ring better than when they train. I'm the exact opposite. Because of fear, my skill level drops at least 20 percent in competition compared to training. He, instead, seems to thrive on the adrenaline of competition—it's as if it wakes him up to his full potential. So our matchup is extremely close. The first round turns out bittersweet. By the end of it, I'm clearly ahead on points since I scored with a takedown, some good leg kicks, and a very close submission attempt, but I wasn't able to finish him when I had the opportunity. The second round begins well, but he's a crafty, sneaky actor. When I latch on a guillotine, he makes gargling sounds as if he is getting choked, pushing me to waste much energy trying to finish the choke. In reality, he's defending well, and he's just baiting me into depleting my gas tank. He eventually frees himself, scores with a takedown, and begins an intense attack, trying to pass my guard and throwing strikes from the top.

It's precisely at this point that the evil inner gnome comes out to say hello. The same exact feeling that got ahold of me last time is here again. I am exhausted. Things are not going my way. I am frustrated. Every bone in my body is screaming at me to quit. *You did your best,* the gnome whispers. *It wasn't good enough. Get out now, while you still have all your brain cells.* In a surreal, out-of-body moment, my mind wanders just as my body is defending against a barrage of punches. I picture myself a couple of hours from now. I can see Elizabeth, my wife, greeting me and asking me how it went. I tell her that the match was close, but that I lost.

"How did you lose?" she asks me.

"I gave up because I was too tired and frustrated to go on."

I can picture the expression on her face and that's all the motivation I need. I know right then and there that there will be no quitting today. Maybe I'll lose the fight, but I'll die on the mat before I let my weird vision come true.

So, c'mon Hirai, do your best, because I am not going anywhere.

By the end of the second round, we are clearly tied, with each of us having won a round a piece on points. Our chess match is so even that we are both spent. Without either one giving up an inch, we have both been forced to expend an ungodly amount of energy. I can barely stand straight. At a rapid assessment of the situation, panic hits me. I haven't been able to put him away early in the fight when I was fresh, and now I am clearly fading faster than he is. Things are probably going to turn uglier in the third round—with the two most likely outcomes being that he'll either control me and win on points, or I'll be too tired to defend well, and his strikes will force a referee stoppage. Neither one looks appealing. My mind races as fast as a damn computer scrolling through all the available options. And suddenly, the only possible positive scenario appears just a few seconds before we are due back in the ring. The plan is clear: I'm going to put every last ounce of strength I have into the first five seconds of the fight. I'll fake a overhand punch, and when he defends, I'll shoot a double leg under his defense, take him down, and try to work my top game well enough to win a decision.

The bell rings, he comes out aggressively, and things unfold exactly as I have seen them in my mind. I fake a power punch that forces him to cover up. I dive for his legs, and by the time he realizes my punch was a feint, his back is already on the ground. The next few minutes will feel like riding a bull. He goes crazy trying to submit me, sweep me, or get back on his feet, since he knows that the takedown has put me ahead on points. But I don't let him. Not today. By the time they announce that I won by unanimous decision, I shake hands with him, and immediately lay down. People come to congratulate me and pat me on the back, but I can't even see them. I just lay there in the ring belly down, sprawled out with my face glued on the mat and my arms stretched as if I was crucified. I literally can't move anymore. I have left every last drop of my energy in the fight. It will take me more than twenty minutes before I manage to sit up.

People who haven't spent plenty of time training may have even been left wondering why we were so tired by the end. We were in good shape and nothing spectacular had happened, so where did all that energy go? It's because we fought nonstop for every inch, in a war of attrition without a second to catch our breath. And in my case, there's also the fact that fear makes me tense up, forcing me to use more strength than necessary. All I know is that I have never been as tired in my life as on that day, and I hope to never be as tired again.

From a technical standpoint, it was an ugly fight. We were too evenly matched, and we ended up nullifying each other's strengths. There was definitely nothing pretty about it. It was a brutal, grindy business. I will not remember this fight for some amazing technique that I pulled off, or because I dominated. In a sense, even the fact that I won the match is secondary. One less takedown and it would have been his hand being raised. As good as winning feels, that's really not what it was about. The reason why I'll remember this fight forever as the one I am most proud of is because it was all about guts—those very same guts that I so shamefully didn't show the last time. I gave everything I had in me, and then some more—without any thought of life before or after this moment, without even caring anymore about getting hurt or about self-preservation. I feel like for once in my life I got to sink claws and teeth into the very heart of fighting. And even the fuckin' gnome was temporarily silenced by this.

I'd love to think that through this fight I turned a corner and heroically defeated the ghosts of fear forever. After all, this is the type of story I have loved in every other martial arts movie ever made: the wimp who faces difficulties but turns himself into a hero through hard work and lives happily ever after. But I know better than that. It's not quite such a straightforward process. Pretending otherwise would be a lie. The truth is that

I defeated fear today. Tomorrow, in the same situation, I may not be able to pull it off. I may crumble and get crushed by the pressure. The reality is that we start over from scratch every day.

Well . . . maybe not exactly from scratch. Once you have experienced facing your weakness and defeating it, it becomes a tiny bit easier to remember how to get there the next time. But it's very far from guaranteed that you'll live up again to your best moments. My friend Mike V (a true god of pro-skateboarding) once told me how he expected that eventually all the fighting (metaphorical and not) would lead to his being able to relax and live beyond conflict. It was only years later that he came to the same conclusion that's now staring me in the face: fighting against your own weaknesses never ends. The battle begins anew every day.

CHAPTER 14

Weight Training for
Heart and Mind

"If you are so damn afraid of fighting, maybe there's a good reason. It's violent, bloody, and you can get seriously hurt. Perhaps you should listen to your instinct. If you don't fight, you'll have no reason to be afraid. It's that simple."

I wish it were that simple. The objection seems logical but, as abstract logic often does, in the end it misses the point.

If you have never experienced pure terror, if you have never embarrassingly lost your emotional balance, if Fear never humbles you by making you well acquainted with your breaking point, then . . . you are in serious trouble.

The day will come when terror will knock on your door and present a bill with interest. Sooner or later, something will happen that will introduce you to all those ugly feelings you have so carefully avoided until that point. And when it does, it will not be pleasant or pretty. Maybe it will not happen in a ring—if you are uncommonly tough and unfazed by fighting—but it will happen.

Willingly putting yourself in a situation in which you'll be pushed far out of your comfort zone, then, is a way to train yourself to regain your balance. The more used you become to bouncing back from the edge of the abyss, the more you will be able to face greater and scarier challenges.

Consider the following story about George S. Patton—the same Patton who was to become one of the greatest American generals of the 20th century. (And, incidentally, the same Patton to whom the following—possibly apocryphal—gems of poetry are attributed: "No bastard ever won a war by dying for his country. He won it by making the other poor dumb bastard die for his country." And even more memorably, "Even though I walk through the valley of death I fear no evil, for I am the meanest motherfucker in the whole valley!") It is said that when he fought his first battle, he was temporarily paralyzed with fear. The shame of this feeling was so intense that the only way Patton shook himself out of it was by choosing to die right then and there. The second he decided to charge the enemy and embrace death, fear was gone. After finding himself still alive at the end of the battle, Patton made use of this experience. He had learned that despite his training and illustrious military ancestors, he was vulnerable to panic. So, he figured that the best cure was to expose himself to fear and danger on a regular basis.

When you want to grow stronger muscles, you lift increasingly heavier weights. The same goes for your metaphorical fear-defeating muscle. If you face often enough increasingly scary forces trying to trample your spirit under their hooves, you can develop the fortitude and resilience to handle emotions that would have otherwise crippled you. It's weight training for your mind and heart. If you never face them, the first time you are forced to confront them, you may get crushed. So, seeking precisely those tests that scare you the most is not as suicidal or as masochistic as it may seem at first. There's nothing secret and esoteric about it. Forging a warrior spirit is the natural result of constant practice.

Absolute fearlessness probably doesn't exist. Much in the same way in which human muscles can only lift so much weight, our spirits can only handle so much pressure. If you apply enough pressure, anyone cracks. In a great book by my friend Sam Sheridan, *The Fighter's Mind*, Sam quotes MMA guru Greg Jackson on this point, "Everyone will break—there's not a man alive that can't be broke. Your job, with all that mental training, that suffering, is just to push your own line of mental breaking so far back your opponent can't find it." If we move outside of the limited sphere of fighting, the "opponent" we are talking about is not a flesh-and-blood human being, but all of life's sources of tragedy and heartbreak. (By the way, when it comes to weird quotes Greg Jackson could have given Patton a run for his money, considering he once confessed, "Ever since I was a kid I always wanted to wrestle a dinosaur.")

I didn't know it at the time, but this is exactly what I tried to do in the following years (in case you are confused, I'm not referring to wrestling a dinosaur, but to facing increasingly more intense levels of fear). Knowing all too well that certain challenges would break me, I carefully picked my fights. The criterion was that I wanted fights that would push me within one inch of quitting, but not beyond that. I ended up winning most of my matches, but wins and losses are always relative to the level of competition you are facing anyway. Ultimately, the outcomes were not all that important. What counted was that this is how I—very slowly—began to improve how I handled fear.

CHAPTER 15

The Drunken Taoist and the Power of Weirdness

"The most potent thing in war is unexpectedness." This piece of advice comes to us thanks to a guy who made a habit of drowning his enemies in rivers of blood. The image may be a bit over-the-top-gory, but the point is the man knew what he was talking about. His name was Julius Caesar, and crushing enemies was his business.

"By steering away from tradition, you'll often catch your opponent off guard." The concept is clearly the same here. This sentence, however, is not from a Roman general who has been dead for over 2,000 years, but from MMA legend Fedor Emelianenko.

The quotes could keep coming, but I'll spare you. Anyone who is intimately familiar with conflict can appreciate this idea. If you fight following the same techniques and tactics used by everyone else, success boils down to who's fresher, stronger, faster, and who has spent more time training for this moment (and, of course, being lucky also helps). But if you want to have an edge over your opponent, you have to drink deeply from the wellspring of weirdness, since he can't prepare a defense against the unexpected. This is why unorthodox techniques and tactics can work miracles.

Before we go on, a quick disclaimer: in order to become a master of the unorthodox, you need to know the orthodox very well. There are no shortcuts about this. You can't just expect to make up for a complete lack of skills in the essential elements of the game through some flashy, weird tricks. In MMA this means you need to be well versed in the standard curriculum in wrestling, striking, and submissions, in addition to developing great cardio, strength, and general athletic skills. But chances are that, across the ring from you, you'll run into somebody who has trained just as hard to develop those same skills, so the odds are annoyingly even. Since I am not a big fan of fighting fair, I make it my specialty to travel away from the beaten path and enlist everything that's weird and unorthodox as my ally. The element of surprise, in fact, often turns out to be the X factor that may tilt the odds in your favor. And whereas there are hundreds of excellent instructors who can teach the foundations of the game, few are those who make their home in the house of weirdness.

This is why good old Leo Hirai asked me for advice when he made his professional MMA debut for the Shooto organization. Facing him had forced me to dig deep inside myself. And I had grown as a person as a result of it. Plus, he was a great training partner—very skilled and ready to push the pace, yet always careful not to injure his teammates. So, shortly after our fight, we began training together, exchanging ideas, and constantly experimenting with new techniques.

"You are like the old drunken Taoist from kung fu flicks," a training partner once told me. "The one who looks like some harmless dude who likes to drink too much . . . When at some point in the movie he runs into a tough, muscular, young challenger whose skills look amazing, no one gives him a chance. But before anyone can understand what happened, the young guy is taking a nap, knocked out cold. You're the same, man. You don't look all that impressive, and you fight differently from anyone else. But then you are the only guy I know who can beat fighters who are much better than you. And no one can understand how you do it. Kind of like Yoda in *Star Wars*: he doesn't look intimidating but he never runs out of tricks up his sleeves. And not that this has anything to do with martial arts, but—like Yoda—you speak a funky brand of English too."

Even though I am not sure if being compared to old drunkards and to two-foot-tall, green creatures with fuzzy ears qualifies as a compliment, he had a point. I had crafted my entire martial arts game around my many limitations. Playing along with the Yoda thing, any time people who couldn't figure out how I had overcome their physical advantages would ask me about it I'd reply, "Jedi mind tricks."

And so Jedi mind tricks were what Leo wanted from me. He had excellent coaches who had prepared him in the orthodox stuff, but he still wished to improve his odds with a touch of something else. On the mats in my garage, we trained ring tactics and developed a game plan. And of course we went over one of my favorite techniques—leglocks. Looked down upon in most Brazilian jiu jitsu schools, leglocks tend to catch by surprise even experienced grapplers because few people specialize in them. Plus, unlike other submission techniques, they can be applied from just about anywhere—it is not necessary to first gain a dominant position. For these reasons, Leo loved leglocks almost as much as I did, so our training sessions would often turn into epic leglock battles.

"Everybody has a plan until they get punched in the face."
The ghost of Mike Tyson and his street wisdom reared its head within the first three seconds of Leo's pro debut. Against my advice, he had decided to test the waters by letting his opponent take the initiative in a stand-up exchange, and heavy leather found his face before the echoes of the opening bell had died down. Once that happened, Mike Tyson's theory proved immediately true. The game plan I had suggested went down the drain, as Leo was too overwhelmed to go back to it. In the second exchange, his opponent (an excellent fighter who would eventually end up squaring off with UFC title challenger and Shooto champion Caol Uno, and a student of UFC veteran Mike "Joker" Guymon) landed even heavier strikes, finishing a combination with a good head kick. This was definitely not the ideal way to begin one's pro career.

Leo's girlfriend was sitting next to me, and was rightfully freaked out by what she was witnessing.

"Is it as bad as it looks?" she asked, clearly begging me to lie to her.

Being Italian, I had no problem obliging. "Not at all," I said. "Those strikes have no power behind them. Leo's barely feeling them."

Of course, I was lying through my teeth. I thought there was a 50 percent chance that Leo would get knocked out within the next thirty seconds.

In full survival mode, Leo tried to take the fight to the ground, but his opponent countered the takedown attempt, landing on top. And in case being outstruck and outwrestled wasn't bad enough, it was clear that his opponent's jiu jitsu skills were decent enough that it was going to be difficult for Leo to submit him or sweep him from the bottom. Somehow, Leo made it out of the first round alive, but there was no doubt about who was winning. The beginning of the second round looked like more of the same. A pattern was emerging: Leo's defense was good enough that he was probably not going to get knocked out or submitted, but it was almost certain that he was heading for a unanimous decision loss.

Unable to make any of his orthodox training work for him, somehow Leo managed to suddenly remember something we had trained over the last couple of weeks. This was the ultimate Plan B—something to be used only if things were going poorly. In a seemingly suicidal move, Leo let his opponent pass to his half guard, and from there set up my trademark move that I use every single time I train: a leglock that begins from the bottom half guard, when the opponent feels safe and in control, and ends with him tapping the mat while still trying to figure out how we ended up there. Leo executed to perfection, and ended up winning, by heel hook, a match in which he had lost every single second up to that moment.

Once I was done jumping up and down screaming "That's my technique!" and patting myself on the back for what awesome coaching advice I could give, I realized that Leo had done something that I probably would have never been able to pull off. The story of the fight, in fact, is not found in tactics or special techniques. And unlike what I may have suggested until now, it is not about my unorthodox and weird ways. It's about the insane warrior spirit Leo displayed—something for which I would gladly trade all the brilliant tactics in the world. He got beat up for two rounds. Nothing he tried worked. For several minutes, all he experienced in the ring was the pain and humiliation that come from being completely dominated by one's opponent. And yet, through all of this, his willpower never wavered. He remained relaxed, seemingly unaffected by the reality of being manhandled in front of a large, screaming crowd. The fact that things weren't going his way left him unfazed. What he demonstrated with apparent ease in the ring is the exact state of consciousness that I had tried to make mine during my entire martial arts career.

CHAPTER 16

The Wildly Inappropriate Sayings of Leo Hirai

Since I just sang his praises, it seems only fair to have some fun picking on Mr. Hirai. Perhaps I shouldn't. After all, when I shot an instructional DVD about, not surprisingly, leglocks, Leo volunteered to serve as a guinea pig, letting me leglock him for over eight hours of shooting. But I helped him win his fight, so we are even. And plus, I can't pass on this opportunity. The man, in fact, is brilliantly oblivious to the obvious sexual double meanings of the stuff he says while working out—which makes training with him hilarious.

So, here we go with the wildly inappropriate sayings of Mr. Hirai—which I dutifully wrote down after I was done laughing my ass off after various training sessions:

Once, when his opponent was in mount position and Leo could not escape, he looked at me and asked, "How do I get him off?"

At a time when he wanted me to bring him a Pride Fighting Championship DVD that I kept forgetting, he looked at me straight in the eyes and said, "Hurry up and give it to me."

Complimenting me on my technique in the midst of a grappling session, he uttered, "You make it hard for me." I hope he meant to say, "You make it difficult for me to win," or something along those lines, but I can't be too sure.

Explaining that he actually didn't mind working ground and pound striking techniques from inside the opponent's guard, he declared for all to hear, "I like being between a guy's legs."

While teaching a beginner how to join centers in order to do a throw, he offered this tip, "Imagine that there's a hole between his legs and you are trying to stick part of you in it." Needless to say, the beginner never came back to training.

And last but not least, Leo is renowned for speaking out loud the sentence that you never want to hear when you are rolling on the mat with somebody: "You actually grabbed my penis."

CHAPTER 17

Breaking a Good Man's Nose, Cavan Cox and the Advantage of Being Insane, and Other Tales

I had always prided myself on being a good training partner who would never hurt anyone sparring with me. In two decades of martial arts, I still had a spotless record in terms of causing serious injury to any workout partner. And then . . .

I was back in Italy for vacation, and was doing a little sparring with a friend named Giancarlo Serafino. I had just finished mentioning how we should go easy to avoid injuries when the gods decided I was in dire need of a refresher course in the deep truth that sometimes shit just happens. I had him in a typical Muay Thai clinch, and I let a knee fly toward his solar plexus— nothing too hard, just enough to let him know it landed. Good plan, except for the fact that he decided to escape my hold by ducking under. And that's when it became clear why you never, *ever* duck against a Muay Thai clinch: with uncanny timing, he lowered his head enough to make sure that it met my incoming knee face-first. What was supposed to be a soft strike to the midsection turned into a frighteningly hard strike to the face.

I took one look at him and thought, *Shit! I Rich Franklined his nose!* (In case the Rich Franklin reference escapes you, and in case you are not disturbed by the sight of a nose floating freely across someone's face, I suggest you watch Rich Franklin's first encounter with Anderson Silva's knees.) I was positively freaked out. I mean, people across the gym had heard the booming impact of my knee; his nose was broken in the nastiest way possible. I wasn't even the one whose face had been creatively redesigned, and yet I was feeling horrible.

Serafino, however, reminded me of what real men are like. In the midst of blood everywhere and bones sticking out in very wrong directions, he seemed more worried about me feeling bad about breaking his nose than about the nose itself. And without raising his voice above the tone you'd have when entertaining some pleasant guest in your living room, he simply said, "Could you please get me a towel? I don't want to get the mat dirty with my blood." I followed him to the locker room, where he went in front of the mirror and, after a few seconds of examining the fracture, grabbed his own nose and snapped it back in place. As I stood staring at him, he simply asked me if I could please get him a pencil to put up his nostril in order to keep the airway open. Throughout this whole time, he never even seemed mildly disturbed, save for a brief comment indicating how his only worry was how this would affect his notorious success with lovely ladies (very Italian of him . . . I know). Had he asked me to chop off my pinkie yakuza-style, it would have been the least I could do.

Later in the day, as we were discussing our respective approaches to martial arts, he asked me point-blank, "Why do you feel the need to test yourself in competition?"

His question made no sense to me . . . "What do you mean, 'why do I feel the need?' It's more like, 'Why don't *you* feel the need?' Competition is the way you face your fears, isn't it?"

Now it was his turn to seem puzzled by my answer. As we talked, it became clear that fighting didn't scare him even a tiny bit. Since he had been a kid, he had never been too intimidated to stand up for himself and his friends. He had won some and lost some, but even getting beat up never fazed him.

By now I hated him a little. He had conquered spontaneously and with apparently little effort one of those fears that I had been struggling with during my entire life. Whatever sense of guilt I had about breaking his nose vanished in a second. I was so damn envious of his quiet, natural toughness that I was tempted to break his nose a second time.

Unfortunately for my ego, he was not an isolated case. Take another training partner of mine, Mr. Cavan Cox. I didn't know him for long before I came to the conclusion that he was batshit crazy. Or at least that's what I told myself, since I couldn't otherwise explain how someone could be so completely devoid of fear. The man would regularly seek out the craziest mismatches and cheerfully fight against people who were twice his size, or incredibly more skilled than he was. Having his jaw broken during one of these suicide fights and having to drink his food through a straw for weeks as a result of this didn't dampen his willingness to throw down literally anywhere, any time, against anyone. The creators of the movie *300* should have paid him royalties for modeling their characters after him.

Along the same lines, I remember a chat I had with UFC legend Randy Couture about fear. Couture wasn't as reckless and wild as Cox, and yet he seemed equally unfamiliar with the mix of intimidation and terror that I always associated with fighting. Just like his rival Chuck Liddell, Couture thought fighting was fun—nothing to be scared of! Liddell would even take naps before his fight, sleeping like a baby without a worry in the world.

All of these individuals frustrated the hell out of me, since they were living examples of everything I wanted to be and wasn't.

But then, on some level I am almost glad I found something that in dramatic, unambiguous fashion scares the hell out of me. Any time I want to test how I handle fear, I know where to go. What if I weren't afraid of fighting, but the fear of being judged, the fear of getting emotionally hurt, and a million other fears still controlled me in daily life? Those fears are easier to avoid openly, and yet they do massive damage. Worse yet, they accomplish this in camouflage: since they are subtle and move silently, it's easy to barely notice them even while they are controlling you from within. Making them even sneakier is the fact that facing them is uncomfortable, so it's almost an automatic reaction to ignore them, pretending they are not there. After all, why face them at all? Why push yourself to do something that's not going to feel good when nothing is forcing you to do it? If it feels awful to deal with them and yet their presence is barely noticeable, why go through the trouble?

Because they'll cripple your spirit—if you let them.

My fears in the fighting game, instead, are very noticeable: they scream in my face and try to crush me. I can't just ignore them. I can either make the conscious choice to avoid them—with the accompanying knowledge that I am a coward for letting them defeat me—or I can make the equally conscious choice to do battle with them. Pretending they are not there is not an option. They are far too loud for that.

And willingly entering Fear's house when the experience is not just unpleasant but downright terrifying makes it much easier for me to face fear in daily life. I mean . . . am I really not going to face something just because it's uncomfortable after stepping up to fears that nearly rip my heart from my chest?

Paradoxically, being so damn scared makes me more prepared to spar with fear in all other aspects of life. By facing the fear of fighting on a regular basis, I have become more sensitive to fear in general, to the point where I am able to tell when it's controlling me even when it's doing so in less obvious ways. And being aware of a problem is the first step to solving it.

Seen under this light, then, being unafraid of fighting may be a missed opportunity if one doesn't know how to handle their fears outside of the ring.

Either that, or perhaps I just came up with a very flowery justification for being a wimp.

CHAPTER 18

Courage and Love

Roman Stoic philosopher Seneca noted that dying gladiators were the most dangerous opponents of all. In a similar vein, the author of the *Hagakure*, Yamamoto Tsunetomo, wrote, "The Way of the Samurai is a mania for death. Sometimes ten men cannot topple a man with such conviction."

The reason for this is paradoxical, and yet simple. Once a warrior loses any instinct for self-preservation, he switches his focus to one thing and one thing only: to destroy his enemy. His entire being becomes consumed with pure battle furor. Nothing else exists but the unshakeable resolve to kill those who stand in his way. Without the natural desire to survive holding him back, a warrior gains powers unknown by regular human beings. He enters battle with the courage and strength that come from a complete lack of hope and fear.

Think Achilles from the *Iliad*, after the Trojans have the very bad idea of killing his best friend. The news of his death projects Achilles into a state of near madness. By the time he dons his armor and gathers his weapons, he is no longer Achilles. Grief has burned away his identity and his humanity. He is now the incarnation of a demon whose only reason to exist is revenge. Losing everything he loved has given him powers to do anything. Anything—that is—except what he wants most of all: the ability to bring his friend back. And so, the only thing left for him to do—the only thing that will silence temporarily the hellish pain that's ripping him apart—is to gorge in an orgy of blood. When he enters battle, no one will be able to touch him. No one will be able to stop him. He is a force of nature bent on destruction. A monster escaped from the nightmares of the god of war. Before meeting their gory deaths, the Trojans will only have time to curse themselves for the horror they have unleashed.

I bet Tolkien had Achilles in mind when he wrote the battle scene in which Eomer, seeing his king killed and believing his sister to be equally dead, leads his knights on a charge against thousands of enemies. His battle cry before driving his horse toward them is, "Death! Ride, ride to ruin and the world's ending!" Everything looks lost, and nothing he can do seems to ultimately matter. So, filled with the power of those who no longer know hope, he rides to shed as much enemy blood as possible before the inevitable end.

But it is precisely this willingness to die and never see home again that helps Eomer, Achilles, dying gladiators, and manic samurai to be unstoppable. At play here are the same dynamics that make crazy people the scariest ones to fight.

This rage that makes one fearless shows up in many different cultures and historical periods. The berserkers, for example, were Norse warriors who, after an abundant meal of hallucinogenic mushrooms, would run into battle with reckless disregard for their own lives. Or the sash-bearers from the warrior societies of several American Indian tribes: in an effort to fight until death or victory, they would drive a spear through their sash into the ground, thereby making escape and retreat impossible.

The few times when I've had the chance to experience a "berserker moment" in a fight, I have literally felt my body swell up with rage and my pain tolerance go up tenfold. Without any worry of getting hurt, and no longer caring about victory or defeat, I have hunted down my opponent with a type of determination I had never known before.

But what had always frustrated me was that these moments would come to me rarely and beyond my conscious control. Short of actually going insane, how could one call upon this fear-vanishing brand of madness? How to tap into this power at will?

I discovered a clue right before my first professional fight in Italy. The night before the fight, I was on an intercontinental call with my wife, who was back in California at the time. Sensing that I was in a similar mental space as before all my other fights (i.e., one inch away from falling through the jaws of the deepest terror), she suggested I switch perspective about my opponent. "Imagine that he is trying to hurt me," she said . . .

And with those eight words everything changed. Fear didn't entirely disappear, but it was lessened dramatically. Rather than feeling intimidated at the thought of my upcoming bout, I couldn't wait to get in the ring and rip his head off.

This insight had not arrived a second too soon. In fact, whereas in terms of venue, audience, and money, calling the event "professional" required a bit of optimism, my opponent was no joke. He trained five hours a day and made a living teaching martial arts. Unlike me, he ate and breathed fighting all day long. Focusing on a couple of advantages on my side (i.e., his lack of good takedown defense and his fighting at a heavier weight class than his natural weight) had helped me to somewhat manage fear, but not nearly as well as I would have liked. Contrary to most of my opponents in smoker fights, this guy was a top-notch athlete and an excellent student of the game. But none of that mattered now. Talking with Elizabeth had pushed a button inside of me, and made me ready, even eager, to clash with him. The ringing of the bell marked the first time in all my time in martial arts that I entered a fight relatively free of fear.

The fight itself was somewhat anticlimactic. The second he threw the first kick toward me, I shot a double leg and took him down. It was clear immediately that he was quite skilled on the ground, and particularly good at escaping. After he defended very well against a couple of leglock attempts, I switched strategy and played a slow, stifling game, utilizing my strength to smother him. Eventually, I passed the guard, and took top mount. From there, I wrapped one arm around his neck and began some ground and pound. My opponent was not the type to quit, but luckily, seeing that there was going to be no escape or defense against my attack, the referee mercifully decided to stop the fight in the first round, giving me my first (and only) victory by ground and pound.

Even though it is safe to say that the fight was definitely not the most exciting to watch, it was then that I began to take giant strides toward discovering the antidote to fear.

Neither pride nor any other personal motivation ever injected me with the necessary courage to stare down fear. My willpower was strong enough to push me to step into the ring despite terror, but not enough to do so unafraid. Over the years, I had tried everything, and none of it had worked long term. What had escaped me all along was that, in the end, defeating fear boils down to love. In this case, it wasn't even like Elizabeth's well-being was actually threatened. But just the thought of it was more than enough to switch my mindset, because sometimes you can do for those you love what you'd never have the energy to do for yourself. Look at it this way: no one in their right mind would ever casually enter a room where an armed serial killer is on a rampage. Now imagine that the person you love the most is trapped in that very room, and suddenly you'd tear down the door to face off against what, until a second earlier, you were running away from. Maybe it's different for other people. Maybe they are braver than me by nature. Or maybe something else does it for them. But for me, the only place from which I can muster courage is the love for those who have given me their heart and soul. As it turns out, a love that nearly hurts 'cause it's so intense is the only force that speaks louder than self-preservation.

CHAPTER 19

Hoka Hey

When I think of the pinnacle of technical achievement in the martial arts among those I have trained with, a few names come to mind—guys like Tim Cartmell, Takahiro Okawa, or Einhard Schmidt. When grappling against them, I have never felt like I was being outmuscled. Without using an ounce of excess strength, they would toss me across the room pretty much at will and with no apparent effort. In some cases, I was even physically stronger than them, and it wasn't like I was a beginner completely devoid of technique. And yet, I was utterly powerless. Losing to them was almost an honor, since I had the best seat in the house to witness pure mastery at work: their opponents' bodies were the canvases used to create masterpieces. From a technical standpoint, they embody exactly what I aspire to become. But as much as I am in awe of their talent, the most amazing technical skill is a very distant second to what interests me most in the martial arts.

Here's a story for you.

On this particular day, a master of tea ceremony in the retinue of Lord Yamanouchi was educated on the difference between image and reality. Because of his status, he was supposed to dress like a samurai, despite knowing nothing of combat. So, when he was challenged to test his skills by a real samurai in the streets of Edo, he began sweating bullets. In an effort to buy time, he asked and obtained to postpone the duel until the following day. Honor dictated he couldn't refuse the challenge, and yet there wasn't a chance in hell that the outcome of the duel would leave him anything but dead. Lacking any clear option, he decided to dedicate the twenty-four hours before the appointed time for the duel to learning what he could about sword-fighting. A quick trip to the closest fencing school dashed any unrealistic hope he might have harbored. The head master told him that there was nothing he could teach him in such a short time that would help him win. Accepting the inevitable, the tea master begged for help in dying honorably. The fencing master agreed only on the condition that the tea master prepare a tea ceremony for him. As the tea master became engrossed in his art, he nearly forgot about the duel and his fear of death. At this point, the fencing instructor interrupted his soon-to-be-dead guest. "You are in the perfect state of mind," he told him. "Keep this presence and spirit during the preparations for the duel, and you'll certainly die well." When the appointed hour finally arrived, the tea master was able to channel that same state of mind, and with perfect composure and lack of fear, he unsheathed his sword. The rival samurai took one good look at him, apologized, and called off the fight.

That's the essence of martial arts right there. Learning how to die is the name of the game.

The classic of Bushido known as the *Hagakure* calls that mindset the "rainstorm attitude." "When caught in a sudden shower, one may determine not to get drenched, running as fast as one can or trying to thread one's way under the eaves of houses along the way—but one gets wet nonetheless. If from the outset one is mentally prepared to get wet, one is not in the least discomfited when it actually happens. Such an attitude is beneficial in all situations."

Everybody loves the martial arts for the sense of empowerment that they offer. The promise that, by developing flawless technique, you'll turn into an undefeatable fighting machine is as seductive as it gets. There's something deeply satisfying about it. On the surface, martial arts dangle in front of our noses this dream of forging the self-confidence of a consummate winner. Just visualizing this is enough for our egos to begin swelling. It's what we have worshipped in every martial arts movie ever seen: the wimp who, through tireless discipline and unyielding willpower, reinvents himself into a heroic warrior, never tastes defeat again, and lives happily ever after.

I have nothing bad to say about this dream. Its appeal is undeniably beautiful. And this desire for self-empowerment is both legitimate and to be encouraged.

This is great and all, but it's not where you will find the raw heart and soul of martial arts.

For me, the essence of the game is found in losing, in *learning how to take a beating.*

Everyone will experience loss and disappointment on and off the mat. Most people will try to shake off this most unpleasant feeling as fast as they can because it's ugly and uncomfortable. Many got into martial arts precisely in order to never have to feel it again. Unfortunately, they are missing the point, because these are the moments when martial arts can teach you the most about yourself and about life. The perfect armbar or the most beautiful spinning kick is of limited use in the rest of life, away from the ring. Learning how to stay with it, when your mind is screaming at you to give up and run as far away as you can, is as fundamental in life as it is inside the ring. Fighting your heart out even when you have no realistic hope of winning is not a skill that's only useful in combat.

Life's own DNA dictates that you will get hurt over and over again, as long as you draw breath. There are no exceptions. Rejection, heartbreak, old age, sickness, and death knock on everybody's door. Similarly, everyone who enters the ring will eventually get mauled. Defeat is not an unfortunate event. Both in combat and in life, defeat is a guarantee. It may show up more or less often. It may take longer than average to find you. But the outcome is never up for debate.

Hoka Hey, the Lakota battle cry, is born from this realization. It may seem curious and self-defeatist to enter battle screaming what is usually translated as "Today is a good day to die." Why not some kickass, macho threat instead? Why not some ego-boosting proclaim of your certainty to win? That's because no matter how skilled you become, you are eventually going to lose. And even if you ignore it, the fear of losing (which is the fear of death by another name) will still play a number on you. Hoka Hey, instead, acknowledges that you can never fully ensure the outcome of a battle. But rather than letting the prospect of death and defeat freeze you, the Lakota warrior embraces his own ultimate lack of control over life and death. "Today is a good day to die" is the battle cry of those who are not going to stop fighting and giving every last drop of blood they have in their veins until you kill them. Once you have already accepted the possibility of death, what can anyone say to scare you?

In training you are given the chance to learn to keep going through defeat, pain, frustration, and utter lack of control. Even though it may not be the easiest thing in the world to see wonderful opportunities while you are getting punched in the face, this is the most fundamental moment that all of martial arts training is about: figuring out how to remain undeterred when all hope of a good outcome has already left town.

Life, eventually, kicked my ass—just as it eventually kicks everyone's ass. What I am thankful for is that I was already used to getting my ass kicked—courtesy of the martial arts. Learning how to take a beating without letting it break my spirit was hands-down the best lesson I ever gained from the martial arts.

PART II

Life and Death
of a Wonderful
Human Being

CHAPTER 20

How an Incredibly Stinky Man Inspired the Woman of My Dreams to Talk to Me for the First Time

"Is this stuff going to help me if shit goes down for real, or are you just wasting my time?"

In the world of traditional martial arts, this is not exactly the typical way students are expected to start a conversation with their teacher. But there was nothing typical about me. And even less about her.

It is also entirely possible that the actual words she used were considerably more polite than those I quoted, but I'm reading between the lines here, and this was quite obviously the meaning of her question. She was blunt without being rude. The lady just had no time to waste, and I could respect that.

She was also beautiful beyond words—physical perfection in the body of a Chinese woman. And yet, Asian stereotypes didn't apply here. In addition to having obviously missed school the day in which they were teaching Confucian respect for one's teachers, she had built an athletic body that was far from the ideal of frail, delicate femininity peddled in some circles. She embodied the best of feminine beauty—let's make no mistake about it—but she also radiated strength every time she moved. She looked like she would be equally comfortable rocking an evening dress and fighting off a mountain lion. She was the perfect Tao, and she was right in front of me!

And speaking of Tao, I seriously dug the only small tattoo she sported: a very yang tiger jumping out of a very yin heart.

Many replies to her question floated in my mind, but I had to struggle long and hard to find one that didn't sound like "Even though I just met you, I love you madly." I had known her for two weeks by then, and I had been obsessing about her for . . . well, two weeks. So, let's rewind to how I met this insanely beautiful, blunt woman.

I was twenty-four years old. Six years earlier I had left behind most everything I had known and abandoned Italy with a one-way ticket to Los Angeles. Italy was a great place to visit and have a good time. But for anything else, it was an old country, where heaviness and stasis ruled. Cynicism was the standard Italian answer toward any attempt at shaking things up. As soon as anyone had a new idea, they'd run into ten people who would tell them right away why it couldn't be done. The option of spending the rest of my existence in Italy felt stifling—cages and obstructions everywhere I turned.

At eighteen, I could already see the rest of my life. All around me were kids who resented the prevailing negativity as much as I did, but felt powerless to change it and were too afraid to leave. After a rapid assessment of my situation, I voted against joining their ranks. Maybe I was making a huge mistake and I'd pay dearly for it. Maybe I'd end up much worse than had I never left. That's ok. I preferred taking that chance to accepting defeat without even having fought a battle. I may have been a wimp in several aspects of my life, but I wasn't about to raise a white flag at eighteen years old. Moving to the US was not a barrel of monkeys, but it offered more risks and more possibilities. I had no idea what things would look like the following month, and I liked that.

Now six years later, after taking my sweet time in community college, I had just graduated from UCLA at record speed. Lack of money, coupled with a curious UC policy of charging students for each quarter regardless of how many courses one attended, convinced me to take advantage of this by enrolling in more units than any sane person should attempt. And so I was done. Graduated. Woppity fucking wop . . . Despite an insanely high GPA, I didn't feel like I had learned much that was even remotely useful. The only reason why I even attended college (besides being in an environment that put me in close quarters with hot women) was the fact that military service in Italy was mandatory . . . unless one was enrolled full-time in a university. In some countries, military service may not be such a bad option, and one may even learn something useful there, but in Italy . . . crazy waste of time—basically one year spent doing nothing, somewhere far from home, being yelled at by some authoritarian assholes, without even the benefit of the company of lovely ladies. So, I knew I'd probably have to enroll in some graduate program soon, even though I could care less about more schooling.

As I was trying to figure out my next move, I rented a tiny place in Westwood, a short walk away from campus, where I still had a part-time job. Rumor had it that my roommate was a former hitman. I was about to use his name now, but why take chances? It was probably all bullshit, but the legend was an article of faith among our friends. What was certain was that he possessed some skills that most law-abiding citizens usually don't feel the need to have in their repertoire. In any case, he was clean, polite, and never brought dead bodies home. And that was good enough for me.

After over a year of calling the poor lady who ran the recreation classes at UCLA every week, my diligence had finally paid off. Probably tired of my stalker/bulldog-biting-at-the-ankles persistence, she offered me what I had been after the entire time: a chance to teach martial arts at the John Wooden Center, UCLA's glorious gym. Just when it looked like the opportunity might never materialize, the phone finally rang and the deal came through.

And so, with my trusted roommate/possible hitman at my side, I made my way to my first day as the head instructor of a new martial arts program. I was as excited as I could be. I'd be teaching San Soo, a type of kung fu with a particularly bad attitude. The room they reserved for me was not exactly designed for martial arts (a racquetball court with some mats thrown in there at the last minute), but I wasn't about to whine. More challenging, though, was what awaited me once I opened the door.

Three things hit me at once. Hit #1: I had expected ten people to show up, and instead I had fifty—way more than the room could comfortably hold. My brain immediately kicked into overdrive, trying to figure out how to run a class under these circumstances. Hit #2: Damn, it stunk in there! As I would find out within a few minutes, the stench came to us courtesy of a guy who considered showers and deodorant as his sworn enemies, and tank tops as his best friends. Hit #3: In an effort to survive the atrocious smell emanating from Mr. Stinky (whose nationality will go unmentioned for the sake of not indulging in stereotypes), my future wife approached me asking if we could keep the door open. Hits #1 and #2 were suddenly off the radar. Hell . . . everything else on earth was off the radar at that moment. It wasn't just because she was a vision of beauty from a better world. Something about her energy was mesmerizing. She was a sun, able to brighten and warm up any room she walked into.

CHAPTER 21

Bruce Lee Taught Me That Love Trumps Stupid Rules

All the reasons why I ever loved martial arts practice . . . well, now I had another one that overshadowed all others. The disconnection between what I was doing and what I was feeling couldn't have been greater. Externally, I was going through the motions of being a focused martial arts instructor. I was teaching my students some rather brutal techniques, and yet all I cared about was melting into the many smiles she sent my way. My actions projected manly toughness and martial prowess, but these were a thin cover disguising that inside I was turning into a giddy, unicorns-and-rainbows-drawing, flying-cupids-dreaming little girl experiencing her first crush. Eye gouges had never been this sweet!

But a pesky rule kept trying to spoil my bliss by reminding me I was a bad, bad man. It is, in fact, pretty much universally accepted that teachers are not supposed to hook up with their students. So my being insanely in love shortly after walking through the door on the first day was making me flunk Teacher Ethics 101 at record speed.

Technically, I could try to bypass the moral dilemma by appealing to the fine print.

Whereas professors who have sex with their students can end up with their heads stuck on a skull rack outside of the college dean's office (because of the possible abuses of the power dynamics inherent in such relationships), my case was different. My classes were not part of the university curriculum. I didn't pass or fail anyone since there were no grades involved in recreation classes. Purists would still consider this a bullshit excuse since teacher-student power dynamics are not limited to grading, but I had never been a fan of being a stickler for rules, and I wasn't about to start in the midst of an elaborate flirting game with the hottest woman I had ever met. Plus, I had the blessing of the patron saint of martial arts—good old Bruce Lee. Lee, after all, ended up married to Linda Caldwell, one of his very first students. Since this was apparently good enough for Bruce Lee, it was good enough for me. Love trumps all rules. And if moralizing devotees of rigid regulations couldn't appreciate this, they could just go fuck themselves.

So, with a prayer to Bruce Lee's spirit to watch over me, I began shamelessly courting her. After class, I found myself coincidentally (well . . . ok . . . not exactly coincidentally . . .) walking home along the same road she walked.

Plenty of attractive women are no longer so attractive when you are close to them. I am not referring to suddenly noticing physical flaws you hadn't noticed from afar. I am speaking of those cases when their physical beauty remains unchanged, but their words and energy prove to be major turnoffs. This is clearly me being picky—I know. The average guy is perfectly satisfied with any good-looking woman as long as she has a pulse (and even that's a preference more than a requirement), so my losing interest in objectively hot women because of their "energy" may sound like some hippie crap. And it quite possibly is. But it's very real to me.

In any case, no such problem presented itself here. Chatting with her was like surfing on top of smiling dolphins. Exhilarating, exciting, electrifying, and some other cool verb that begins with the letter E. We talked about everything and more: from the philosophy of Henry David Thoreau to street fights; from the deepest life priorities to burp jokes; truly life, the universe, and everything. But as fun as the content of the conversation was, it was little more than an excuse for something else that was passed invisibly when we were close. I loved what she said, but I loved even more that special "something" that was dancing around her skin.

A week later it was becoming obvious that our bodies were on a collision course with each other. The life expectancy for whatever force was stopping us from diving into each other's arms and kissing wildly was grim. One night, aching to hear her voice, I called her up. I had nothing special to say. I was just dying to feel a step closer to her. Six hours of phone conversation later we had covered just about every topic known to man. By that point it was 5 AM, and we were half asleep and half still talking. Out of the blue, the crazy woman asked, "I wanna go for a walk. Are you coming with me?" There was more than a hint of amused challenge in her voice. I was already under my blankets, drifting into dreamland, and every muscle in my body was begging me to say "no way," but I knew this was a test and backing down was not an option. And so, out of bed I went.

Less than half an hour later I was standing under her window. She came down to meet me in the street; she was so damn beautiful even in the goofy pajamas she wore on our walk. No mind-blowing sex ensued. Just ridiculously tender walking hand in hand, watching the sun rise, and returning to her place to catch the greatest film in the history of moviemaking (*The Princess Bride*—in case you had any doubts). And then it was time for the new day to begin. By the time I arrived at my job, the silliest smile in the world had parked itself on my face and refused to leave. I was supposed to tutor some poor UCLA students in . . . something—it could have been Italian or history or religion or just about anything else since I wore a million hats and made it my specialty to be knowledgeable enough in any field under the sun. Regardless of what the now-forgotten field actually was, my eyes were pretty much shut closed and the odds of me doing a decent job were less than zero. Lucky for me, my first students of the day were a couple of women who were highly sympathetic to my romantic adventures, so I dodged a bullet and didn't get fired. Not that I would have cared after a night like that.

Just when everything was going right, I was the one to throw a wrench into what looked like an impending relationship. Since we were putting all our cards on the table, I felt it was only right to inform the woman of my dreams that I thought monogamy was bullshit. I probably phrased it a bit more elegantly and offered my best philosophical defense for open relationships, but basically that was my message. Rather than freaking out and running in the opposite direction, she was very cool about it. Philosophically, she was on board, but she knew herself too well to actually go for it. She knew that if she accepted it, she'd struggle with it the entire time. So, with great honesty, she put the ball back in my court, "If that's what you want, I respect it and wish you the best, but not with me. If you want a relationship with me, it's only with me."

In other words, you can either follow your philosophy of relationships or you can have me—not both. The choice is yours. I've met a million people who verbally defend the integrity of monogamy only to cheat in actual practice. That was never an option for me. Once I give my word, I never break it. Ever. For any reason. And so I thought about it long and hard for a full 0.2 seconds before jumping headfirst into it. All I wanted was her. Let my philosophical ideals about relationships be damned.

CHAPTER 22

From the Pits of Hell

"The only reason why you were born is that we didn't have enough money for an abortion."

Not exactly the message that any fourteen-year-old girl would want to hear from her father. But then again, there was nothing about life in the Han household that any fourteen-year-old girl would want to be part of.

Had her father been completely honest, he should have probably added that the other reason they didn't abort her was because she was the only one in the family to be born on American soil—thereby the only US citizen in a family of illegal immigrants. The father was from mainland China. The mother, three sisters, and one brother were all born in Taiwan. Elizabeth—this was the name of the lady of my dreams—was the father's insurance ticket. Even if he got busted by Immigration, he probably wouldn't have been deported since he was the only provider for a US citizen. If you think this is cynical and fucked-up, it's but an appetizer for the rest of Elizabeth's childhood.

By the time I met her when she had just turned twenty-four, she shone with an inner and outer beauty that made it impossible not to notice her. But she came from the deepest darkness, and traces of that darkness would never fully leave her, no matter how hard she tried to shake them off. About four years before I met her, she had decided that, since she was emotionally in a better state by then, it would be a good idea to face her past. The noble experiment of a few weeks of therapy trying to grapple with her childhood ended up with Elizabeth holding a razor blade in a warm bathtub while contemplating the old Hamletic question. After this, she decided that perhaps certain doors were better left closed.

She came from a place where horrendous physical and mental abuse was an everyday occurrence. I'm not exactly sure what parenting book her father consulted, but certainly it was one that strongly recommended equal measures of mind-fucking manipulation and ultra-bloody beatings as the twin pillars of the kind of good parenting any child needs. Her mother, who was never a strong person to begin with, eventually went completely insane. There is some debate on whether she was made crazy by the regular beatings or whether she was heading that way on her own, but the end result was the same. Ditto for Elizabeth's only male sibling: her brother would also grow up diagnosed as clinically schizophrenic with the extra bonus of being prone to extreme violence. All the sisters would develop psychological issues of differing severity resulting from their childhood. Some of them would still manage to shape a good life for themselves despite this, but getting out of the Han household unscarred was simply not an option.

By the time Elizabeth was fifteen, she started hitting the weight room in an effort to turn her body into a source of strength rather than pain—much to the chagrin of her father. By the time she was sixteen, she became a ward of the court and ran away from home—never to see her parents again.

Her older sisters offered to let her live with them so she could go to college close to home, in the San Francisco Bay Area. The gesture was definitely sweet. Staying with them would have been the logical, safe choice. But Elizabeth was not one to play things safe. The second she was done with high school, she decided to leave everything behind and create her own path far from anyone's influence. So, she packed her bags and made her way to UCLA.

Seventeen years old, in a city where she knew no one, insecurity and loneliness stalked her daily, but she hit them back harder than they hit her. For better or worse, this was the forge where she would build her spirit. By the time I met her, one of her defining characteristics was a near-maniacal commitment not to let fear or pain stop her from doing what she wanted. Hell . . . Nietzsche would have found her willpower intimidating. I may have been the martial arts teacher, but she was a warrior through and through.

And yet she wasn't stupid. She was conscious that as much as she had taken giant steps to move away from her past, she could never fully escape it. A relationship with her meant entering a minefield—she made no mystery of this. If anything, she tried to warn me away, or at the very least make me fully aware of what I was getting into. Not for a second did she try to pose as someone she wasn't, or paint things better than they were. She laid all her cards on the table and told me from the start that being with her was not going to be easy.

What could be so difficult about loving a woman of maddening beauty who loved me back as intensely as I loved her?

Elizabeth was two people. Her nature exuded warmth and kindness. She had a huge heart and an inner fire that made random strangers fall in love with her in an instant. Dogs and babies would drop anything they were doing as soon as they saw her, and inexorably found themselves gravitating toward her, as if she were the sun, and they were the planets rotating around her. She was a walking, high-octane concentrate of passion and determination. She owned any room she walked into. Her laughter . . . her laughter was pure, unrestrained joy, spreading the contagion of happiness to those within earshot.

But this was not all that she was. The other person that lived within her was the product of a fucked-up childhood—unforgiving, merciless, ever ready for a fight. She came from hell, so trusting anyone was for her a titanic struggle.

"Anger is the emotion I'm most comfortable with," she told me several times, and she wasn't lying. It's as if her sunny nature and her tortured upbringing were constantly waging war against each other.

Nearly everyone would be captivated by her magnetic personality. But people regularly pissed her off, and she would waste no time pushing them away. Without saying a word, she could express her disgust with you in a way that made you want to crawl back into a hole and never poke your head out again. The fury in her eyes could set you on fire. The intensity of her energy didn't change. Both sides of her were equally strong, but one could make you touch the sky while the other would crush you to pieces.

On paper, it looked like a bad match. Among the many things that made us incompatible: I was a happy puppy who thrived on sharing my house with friends and having people over in a "the more, the merrier" kind of way. She grew up locking herself in the closet to play with some toys, since that was the only place where she felt safe. Needless to say, this left her with a bit of a heightened sense of privacy. Whereas I loved to share my space, her priority was protecting it. I wanted a tribe.

She wanted to be left the fuck alone. Living together was not going to be simple for us.

She told me all this right off the bat. She also told me that she survived her upbringing through sheer willpower, but this had left her with a shrunken muscle for compromise. As much as she would have loved to make compromises in our relationship, it was almost certainly not going to be a fifty-fifty deal. She would accommodate me as much as she could, but it might not be that much. In not so many words, she had to have things her way most of the time. In saying this, she wasn't trying to be mean or to dominate the relationship. She was very matter-of-fact about it.

"I have tried to change much about myself, and I have succeeded to some degree, but I think I've hit my limit. I love you, but what you see is what you get. I don't want you to start things under the illusion that 'one day she'll change' because I probably won't. Either you can accept things as they are or you should find someone more compatible."

So there it was—take it or leave it.

Many times over the years, she asked me, "Why do you love me? Don't you think you'd be better off finding someone more like you, someone easier, with less baggage?" It would have probably been much easier, but "easy" was not what I craved. Rather than scaring me away, her raw, disarming honesty made me love her even more. There was no simple, logical answer to *why* I loved her. My love for her had nothing to do with logic. She didn't have to *do* anything for me. Just the fact that she existed and she loved me was all I needed. Without having to lift a finger, she brought me more emotional balance and happiness than I had ever had. I'm sure that I could have found a thousand women more compatible with me, but I doubt 99.9 percent of them could have had the same effect on me.

And so I jumped into the relationship headfirst. No hesitations. No regrets. I wanted to be with her no matter how tough it would be, no matter how much of a struggle or how painful. I loved her so damn much that I was happy to give up pieces of myself for her. Had anyone else told me the same about their relationship, I'd have thought it was a really bad idea. Others close to me were similarly weirded out: however amazing Elizabeth was, our relationship didn't rest on a healthy foundation. After all, I basically lived my life in constant fear of anything that could possibly piss her off, and I was rarely relaxed since I was always trying to anticipate potential problems and defuse them before they got under her skin. Blocking anything that could set off her anger kept me always on edge.

I saw those dynamics, but I didn't care. I knew all that, and still thought it was worth it.

More than anything, I wanted to make her happy. Any time her vulnerability would peek through her tough exterior I felt invested with a responsibility to give her all the love she had never received. After all, I had been showered with affection and attention in my childhood, while she hadn't been. In a perhaps megalomaniac state, I felt like no one else would be able to do it. And she said as much multiple times. "Only you hold the secret to soothing the savage beast in me," she wrote me, only halfway joking. "Your presence provides me with a sense of stability, the only kind I've known. Sometimes you seem to be my only source of joy. Don't give up on me, love."

How the hell could I? I was the only one she'd lower her defenses with. And what I could see in her any time her defenses were down was the kind of tenderness that needs to be protected and showered with love. My mission in life would be to make her happy.

She knew I felt that way, and it worried her as much as it gave her warmth. "You can't save me," she told me over and over again with words that would prove painfully prophetic. "It's not your job to make me happy. Only I can make myself happy."

All true . . . and yet all I wanted to do was to give her everything she deserved and never had.

CHAPTER 23

Doing Tai Chi Outside of a Restaurant in Westwood after Midnight

I am willing to admit that there's a tiny possibility that I was a bit over the top with my overprotective "my mission in life is to make up for all the love you've never had" act. Consider this story.

A few months after our initial meeting, we moved in together. Elizabeth picked up a part-time job waiting tables at a restaurant in Westwood. She often worked nights—when the tips were usually better—and ended her shifts fairly late. I wasn't particularly thrilled with the idea of her walking home alone, so I made a point of picking her up at the end of the night. The problem was that there was no way to predict for sure when she would be done, since it depended on how many late customers had to be pushed out, how quickly everyone cleaned up the place, etc. Problem #2 was the fact that neither one of us owned a cell phone back then (prehistory—I know). So, picking her up at the right time required psychic powers or serious luck. Occasionally, I'd arrive just as she was ready to leave. Much more often, I'd have to wait. And wait. And then wait some more. I didn't mind, though. I'd walk to a mostly deserted alley on the side of the restaurant and go through some Tai Chi forms while I kept an eye on what was going on inside the restaurant. Quite a few times, my Tai Chi, waiting-for-her sessions turned into marathons lasting over an hour.

But it was worth it. Every time she'd walk out and see me there, she'd have the biggest smile on her face. This didn't prevent her from scolding me, "It's sweet you pick me up, but I feel bad about you waiting so long. I'll walk home on my own next time."

Nice try, but no way.

"Alone? After midnight? Hell no. I don't mind waiting for you."

Based on everything I've told you so far, I may come across as reasonable and even chivalrous, but the detail I forgot to mention: the restaurant was barely a block away from our house.

CHAPTER 24

How *Army of Darkness* Saved
My Wedding

"Wanna get married on Monday? My day is clear."

"Monday . . . let me check my schedule . . . yup. Monday works. Let's get married on Monday, then."

Considering that most people in the US dedicate an ungodly amount of time, money, and energy to planning their weddings months ahead of time (if not longer), it is safe to say that our wedding plans were a tad on the weird side. And things were going to get much, much weirder.

We were a couple of years into our relationship by the time we got married. Incidentally, neither one of us was a big fan of marriage, or weddings for that matter. The whole notion of dragging the state with its court-certified documents into our relationship sounded like the furthest from our idea of romance. The meeting of love and bureaucracy didn't seem all that appealing. As far as ceremonies go . . . Elizabeth's enduring break from her parents didn't make her jump with joy at the thought of a traditional wedding. And I, with my pain-in-the-ass nature, always hated formal ceremonies. Hell . . . I had never even attended my own graduations, or anything of that sort, so I wasn't exactly begging her to change her mind due to my deep-seated need to go through a wedding. Had she wanted to, I'd have done it for her in a heartbeat, but since she didn't care, so much the better. We were crazy in love with each other, were ecstatic to be living together, wanted to have kids, and talked frequently about grocery shopping together when we would be in our eighties. We just didn't feel the need to go through the motions to have the state call what we had a marriage.

So, why get married at all?

The truth is we probably would have never gone through with it, except for one annoying detail: we liked the idea of me being kicked out of the country even less than the idea of marriage. After eight years in the United States, I was about to be done with graduate school—which meant that my student visa would be up soon. My legal options for staying in the country were somewhat limited. And marriage was at the top of the short list. So, Elizabeth sensibly decided that marrying me was a sweet alternative to me being deported. We were living our lives basically as a married couple anyway, so might as well get the stupid piece of paper and get Immigration off my back.

And this brings us to that fateful Monday.

By the time we got to City Hall and met the state employee in charge of getting us married, we realized we had forgotten something important.

"Where are your witnesses?" the man asked us.

Elizabeth and I turned to each other with the classic "oh shit" look on our faces. As luck would have it, another couple was waiting to get married after us, and they were equally witness-less (I doubt that's an actual word, but perhaps it should have been one considering that forgetting witnesses seemed like a pretty popular thing to do that day). And so the logical step was for us to serve as witnesses for each other.

I thought we were weird for getting married in City Hall and forgetting witnesses, but we were clearly amateurs compared to the other couple: the man was in his UPS uniform, was trying to get married during his lunch break, and was actually getting a bit antsy about how long everything was taking since he had to clock back in at work as soon as possible.

In case all of this is not weird enough yet, the City Hall employee in charge of performing the ceremonies was a Filipino gentleman with the thickest Tagalog accent on the planet. This fact—coupled with my crazy thick Italian accent—made for interesting proceedings. He had absolutely no understanding of anything that came out of my mouth. I similarly had no idea of what he was saying. The problem was that the stupid wedding ritual required that I recite some arcane formula after him. But when he spoke the first lines I was to recite, all I heard were some weird sounds that may or may not have been words. So I had to ask him to repeat. And so he did. And I had to ask him again. And so he did. And I had to ask him again. And . . . well, you catch my drift.

I looked into Elizabeth's eyes in a panic, silently asking for help. She looked back at me with an equally puzzled expression that was simultaneously saying A) "I have no idea of what he is saying either," and B) "You are on your own here." Swallowing any semblance of dignity (which luckily wasn't much considering I was the guy who forgot to bring witnesses to his own wedding, and who had recruited as a replacement a groom in UPS uniform), I asked to repeat again and again. By now, it was getting embarrassing for both me and the poor Filipino who was probably thinking, *Why doesn't this fuckin' Italian understand a word of English?*

And that's when Bruce Campbell came to the rescue.

Not literally. In case you are wondering, the glorious Bruce, star of countless B-movies, didn't actually break into City Hall to save me from my predicament. What happened was that I remembered a scene from one of the greatest movies in the history of cinema, *Army of Darkness*, in which Bruce Campbell had to recite a formula he couldn't recall and decided to cough his way through it. And so I did the same, mixing what may have been English words with random bouts of coughing. The Filipino dude seemed perfectly satisfied with my creative solution, even though neither of us had any clue what I was saying.

When it came time to wrap things up, he finished the ritual formula informing Elizabeth that I was now her husband (or something to that effect), and told me, "She's your locally wedded wife." Despite my lack of familiarity with wedding traditions, I was pretty sure he was supposed to say "lawfully wedded wife." But apparently he had decided that people who can't even remember to bring witnesses to their own wedding shouldn't be expected to uphold their marriage vows once they crossed county lines.

CHAPTER 25

A Tiger out of the Cage

One of Elizabeth's sisters once told me a story that revealed everything I could want to know about Elizabeth's spirit. She was about four or five years old, and somehow she had done something to upset her sister Belle (admittedly, not a difficult thing to do). Faithfully following the Han family approach to constructively expressing one's anger, Belle grabbed a belt and told her she was going to whip her with it. Belle was considerably older and bigger than Elizabeth, so the wise course of action would have been to run or beg for forgiveness.

Not Elizabeth. She stood her ground, pulled out her own belt, and got ready to throw down. Belle couldn't believe her eyes. Elizabeth was a tiny dweeb, her belt was equally diminutive and didn't even have a buckle—it was little more than a colored piece of string. Surprise mixed with admiration about the smurf's attitude made Belle laugh and forget about her violent purposes (undoubtedly the first time in the history of the Han household that anyone had decided that one's anger didn't require the shedding of someone else's blood).

That was Elizabeth in a nutshell. From very early on, her character was forged with a purpose. In the face of conflict, her attitude invariably was: "I don't care about the consequences. You may kill me but you are not going to bully me." This approach was applied equally toward people in her life, and toward reality in general. It made her fearless with a kind of defiant "I'll laugh in the face of death" crazy samurai spirit.

This was just about one hundred eighty degrees away from my mentality. I regularly calculated everything, analyzing every situation in order to minimize risks. A strong survival instinct pushed me to rely on strategy and quick thinking to increase my odds of success while minimizing danger. Elizabeth, on the other hand, jumped out of airplanes for fun (both literally and figuratively).

The first time we went skiing together I was reminded yet again of whom I was dealing with. I hadn't skied in over a decade but I had grown up doing it. Elizabeth had only gone a handful of times in her life. So, we soberly started out the day on some relatively easy slopes. After only two runs, Elizabeth motioned to me that she wanted to change slopes.

"Let's go down that one."

"That's a double black diamond, sweetie. It's the most difficult slope on the mountain."

"So?"

"You are little more than a beginner and I haven't skied in forever."

"Nah. We'll be all right. I'm bored with the other slope anyway. If we go slow, we can take this one."

My stupid ego got the best of me, and my fear of looking like a wimp in her eyes overcame my fear of the double black diamond. Expecting broken bones and random disasters, I led the way. To my surprise, we survived without fractures or concussions, but I still thought she was nuts.

Nuts or not, her attitude gave her a type of manic confidence that somehow wasn't self-delusion. Results spoke loud and clear. Her attitude truly empowered her to pull off unexpected achievements.

Try this: The gym at Cal State Long Beach, Brazilian jiu jitsu club in session. Elizabeth had trained in jiu jitsu for a grand total of probably twenty times in her life—the last time about seven years earlier. As we warmed up, I gave her a refresher focusing on a couple of sweeps and a single submission—the guillotine choke. Toward the end of the training session, one of the guys running the class decided to pair everyone for a competitive drill: two people at a time would go to the center of the mat and, while everyone else watched, one of them would try to sweep while the other would try to pass the guard. Both could attempt submissions. Most beginners tend to freeze when put on the spot in front of everyone, so I was a bit concerned for how Elizabeth would handle this. Plus, she was paired with a guy who was about fifteen pounds heavier than her, and was nothing but lean muscle. They fought it out intensely for a minute or so, without anyone gaining a clear advantage. She was doing very well, but eventually he set up an excellent sweep. She went airborne on her way to being swept. I was getting ready to compliment her for the good effort when she got back in line, but it wasn't over. Somehow, she regained her balance in midair like a freakin' cat. By the time she landed, she was mad at how close she had come to being defeated. Without losing a beat, she grabbed his legs, tossed them to the side, passed into top mount and locked a guillotine choke that had him tapping in no time. Everyone looked at me with an unequivocal "who the hell is *she*?" expression on their faces. Here was this beautiful, ultra-feminine woman who was not intimidated by being the only female in the room, by being put on the spot, or by her opponent's strength advantage. She was a damn fury, and fought with the spirit of a tiger out of the cage. From a technical standpoint, most people in the room were much better than her. But in terms of fighting spirit . . . good luck matching hers.

I am told that some men would be intimidated by being in a relationship with such a woman. I don't think I understand that. From the second I met her I knew she was more fearless than I could ever hope to be. But so what? The way I saw it, I could learn much from her in that department. She pushed my limits many times, but always in a loving way. And I only improved as a person because of it. She once convinced me to jump on a series of zip lines in Costa Rica. Considering that tall escalators used to be enough to remind me of how much I hated heights, being thrown at top speed several hundreds of feet up in the air on a crazy ride stretched between two mountains wasn't my idea of fun. I looked down and I was so high up that the giant trees below looked like ants. I looked up and saw that the only thing preventing me from falling to my death were two inches of steel cable holding me above the jungle. I hated her during every minute of it. But I also loved her for helping me stretch my comfort zone. It wasn't just about fear of heights. By the time we were back home, I was less intimidated by a myriad of things, more willing to take chances and embrace adventure. And I absolutely loved that feeling.

Despite her crazy fearless persona, and my much more mellow self, ours wasn't the love story of a banshee and a wimp. Fear comes in many forms, and I wasn't awful at dealing with all of them.

"You are the bravest man I know," she told me a few times in a statement that wasn't as contradictory as it may seem, considering all the other times she had teased me about my fears. She was talking about emotional bravery.

"Every other person I know," she added, "spends their lives hiding. They are afraid to show their emotions, afraid of how others will judge them, afraid of finding out who they really are. Even some of the best people in my life are pathologically afraid of getting hurt, and this stunts their ability to love deeply. Being too busy setting up walls and defenses, they always hold something back. You . . . you love with reckless abandon, make yourself completely vulnerable, and never shy away from intensity out of fear of getting hurt."

To be perfectly honest, at the beginning of our relationship I had tried to run the script I had lived by in previous relationships. It went something like this: "I'll listen to your deep-seated insecurities and help you in any way I can, but I will not burden you with the dark emotions haunting me because they are too tough and heavy for anyone else to deal with."

I thought I was being generous, perhaps even chivalrous in this, but Elizabeth saw right through it and called me on it.

"What kind of condescending bullshit is this? You think you are strong enough to handle my problems, but I'm too frail to help with yours? You are the white knight coming to save me, but you don't want to burden the tender princess with your deep, masculine problems? Fuck that. You may think you are trying to protect me, but you are only protecting your own ego. Just be real with me—insecurities and all—or don't be in a relationship with me."

Touché. She was right. So, from that day onward I dropped my act. But I still didn't see what I was doing as "bravery," because I wasn't scared of those things to begin with. I didn't have to overcome anything. It came naturally to me. I was accustomed to getting emotionally hurt, and I was not afraid of it.

If my personality was made of differing parts of fear and bravery, hers was also more complicated than first impressions might have suggested. Even though she was undoubtedly one of the most fearless people I had ever met, other parts of her regularly surfaced. I remember laughing my ass off every time this super-tough woman would wake me up in the middle of the night after she had seen a spider in the bathroom. *A tiny spider? Really? I have to get up to take care of it because it freaks you out?*

Or the fact that if I wasn't with her, she'd stay up until she couldn't hold her eyes open anymore, because—like a kid—she was incapable of relaxing and going to sleep unless her body forced her to. And if I was with her, she wouldn't sleep unless I held her and let her fall asleep in my arms. The fact that she was a tiger out of the cage didn't mean she couldn't also be a little girl at the same time.

CHAPTER 26

Nietzsche Would Have Been
Intimidated by Such Willpower

Sometimes the line separating willpower and insanity is danger-
ously thin. When you stubbornly keep believing you will find a
way, even when all the odds are clearly telling you failure is the
only logical outcome, you are either a giant of self-confidence
or just plain crazy.

When a couple of years into our relationship Elizabeth
shared with me her long-term plans, I really didn't know on
which side of the line she was. After going back and forth on
the decision for a while, she had finally decided she wanted
to go to medical school to become a doctor . . . which was a
sweet concept except for the fact that she had graduated with a
degree in English, and her grades were nowhere near what was
needed to get into medical school. Worse yet, she had earned all
her best grades in humanities, but had either dropped or failed
almost every science class she had taken in college. How the hell
she thought this background could lead her to medical school
was a complete mystery to me. But not to her. She believed she

had done poorly in sciences because she had been completely unfocused—too distracted by the experience of leaving behind everything she knew and being a teenager creating her path from scratch alone in LA. Now that she was in a very different place in her life, she was confident she could pull it off. So, her plan was to go back and take a full two years of science prerequisites before taking the MCAT and applying to medical school.

Again, this sounded sweet but crazy. My strategic mind saw hardly any viable path to get there. How was she going to raise her GPA dramatically while taking super difficult science classes she had failed in the past? It would have been a miracle if she had kept the same GPA in science courses, but a substantial improvement? No way.

I tried to be really gentle in voicing my concerns. I just didn't want her to get her hopes up and be crushed when the inevitable failure would shut the door on her master plan. I loved her to death and wanted to support her, but was also trying to view it realistically.

Fuck off.

In not so many words, this was her response to my objections. "If you don't believe in me, then too bad for you 'cause I'm doing it anyway."

"I believe in you, and will support you every step of the way, even if I don't see how you will pull it off. I don't need to see it. You do. And if you do, I have your back."

An honorable enough compromise—she could live with it.

On a practical level, things would get complicated really quickly. She was accepted to school in Northern California, while I was still doing graduate work in LA. So, this meant Monday through Thursday I would be in LA before heading out to Northern California to spend time with her from Thursday night through Sunday—quite brutal for both of us. The rhythm and traveling were intense enough that by Thursday night I unfailingly developed an epic headache, and Excedrin would become my best friend. As insane as some of this was, there was something sweet about it—as if we were united together in a crazy quest. The days we would be apart, we'd always chat on the phone late into the night, and I would sing her to sleep with Lakota Sun Dance songs.

Sweet or not, part of me wanted to scream, "I told you so" by the time her first graded exams of the semester came back. Low marks across the board. If it had looked nearly impossible from the start, by now she was in a place where she could still mathematically pull it off, but nothing short of absolute perfection would get her there. It was over. It was just a matter of time until she accepted it . . .

Except for the fact that now that her back was fully against the wall, somehow she began to climb out of the hole one inch at a time. It didn't make any logical sense, and yet it was happening. By the end of the semester, she had aced every class. The following semester the same story would begin, with terrible grades on the first exams before she would begin pulling miracles again. Two years and an MCAT later, she was admitted to medical school.

There was barely enough time to pat her on the back for what she had managed to achieve before the challenges intensified further. On my end, the location of her school looked like a welcome surprise since it was in the LA area, but it was so far from my teaching gigs that I spent the following couple of years driving about four hours a day just to get to and from work. And this was child's play compared to what she had to do: between attending classes and studying, she'd work a punishing regimen of about fourteen hours a day. In the midst of all of this, she had transformed herself into an amazing student well on her way to becoming a doctor—just as she had told me.

Her willpower simply defied reason, and my ability to understand. From where I saw things, she was a damn hero.

CHAPTER 27

Giving Birth to a Baby in the Living Room

"Would you mind pissing on another stick?"

"Still not convinced you are pregnant?"

"Just one more time to be sure."

I am fairly confident that if there were a prize for the man who has taken the greatest number of pregnancy tests in history, they would name it after me. In disbelief over the fact that it had taken just a couple of days for her to get pregnant since we decided to try for a baby, Elizabeth kept thinking there was something wrong with the pregnancy kit. Taking the test five times still didn't convince her so . . . "Daniele, would you mind taking one to make sure these things work?"

Damn . . . the weird things you do for the people you love.

As it turned out, those things did work, and she was indeed pregnant.

By now, we had been together for ten years. During that time, I had invented a career for myself as a writer, college professor, and martial arts instructor; and she had willed her way into medical school and gone through internship and residency. Achieving what at the beginning had looked like an impossible goal, however, had been a mixed blessing at best. The reality is that she had hated every minute of the path taking her there. Her approach to medicine clashed dramatically with her training. Prevention, diet, exercise, and a holistic view of the human body were the cornerstones of her vision. But with increasing disappointment, she was finding out that what most medical schools were dealing was a hyper-specialized program dividing health into tiny separate compartments. She knew this going in, but the reality was much worse than she had expected. This type of training was designed to produce doctors that were little more than glorified drug dealers pushing pharmaceutical products to fix one health problem, while often creating a secondary one as a result. So, not surprisingly, she felt like she was swimming against the current the entire time.

By the time it was all over, she had joined a practice focused on osteopathic treatments and preventive care—much more in line with her ideas about health—but she was also completely burned out. The feeling of having been indoctrinated into a worldview she despised combined with the crazy hours she had had to put in (it wasn't unusual for her shifts to add up to eighty hours a week during residency) had depressed her to the core. Whatever energy reserve she once had was long gone. She smiled much less often, was chronically exhausted, and her patience was down to nothing. It was as if med school had sucked out her zest for life. Unsurprisingly, we argued more as the quality of our relationship steadily declined during her time in medical school.

With residency wrapping up, and the next phase of her life ahead of her, it seemed like she was about to resurface after a long time under water. At least she could begin to finally experience things she could be excited about. Having a baby was one of them. We had wanted to for a long time, but it would have been nuts to try when every other minute of her time was taken. Now that it was over, it was baby time. Life was going to be good again, so the timing was on our side.

Her battles with the medical establishment were not quite over yet, though. Actually, being pregnant brought them back up all over again. The more she talked with gynecologists and nurses, the less she liked the idea of giving birth in a hospital. The entire birthing protocol was designed around the comfort and needs of the doctor delivering the baby, and the hospital's desire not to be sued. The insanely high rate of often unnecessary C-sections, the position of delivery, the quantity and quality of drugs involved . . . none of this appealed to her. And when she tried having rational discussions about some of her concerns in an honest doctor-to-doctor fashion, it became clear to her that there was very little negotiating room. Delivery rooms were assembly lines spitting out babies in almost industrial fashion—the McDonald's of birthing.

"Screw it," she said after another frustrating gynecological visit. "Let's have the baby at home."

This was less insane than it may have appeared at first. It wasn't an impulsive, rebellious decision, but rather was the logical conclusion drawn from her understanding of medicine. Working in a hospital for so long had convinced her that a hospital was the last place where she wanted to bring a baby into the world. Plus, she was extremely comfortable with her own body and with everything that giving birth entailed. Having a baby at home with only the assistance of a midwife perfectly fit her barbaric, fiercely independent self.

By the time the ninth month rolled around, we could hardly wait. The ultrasound pictures had revealed that we were going to have a baby girl, and had given us a first glimpse of the adorable alien growing inside of her. Both Elizabeth and I loved the name Isabella, so it was an easy choice, plus I liked the irony of nicknaming a cute tiny girl Iz after Israel Kamakawiwo'ole, a 700-pound Hawaiian musician with the voice of an angel.

The night of July 1, Elizabeth decided to have "a chat" with Isabella. Throughout the pregnancy, we both often "talked" to her thinking and hoping that we could communicate with her somehow. So far it had worked like a charm: once when Elizabeth had not felt her move for hours, she had asked her to kick her a little to let her know everything was ok. Less than a minute later, Isabella kicked. And on another occasion, when the ultrasound had shown that Isabella was turned the wrong way, Elizabeth had asked her to please turn the other way to facilitate the birth. They gave her a second ultrasound shortly thereafter, and Isabella had turned as requested. Coincidences? Probably . . . or maybe not.

Iz was displaying some rather curious behavior while still in the womb, so you never know. With unfailing regularity she would keep kicking if her mom's hand was on the belly, but when anyone else put a hand there, she'd stop immediately. Being her father didn't grant me an exception. She would always freeze as soon as I put my hand on Elizabeth's belly. So, just for fun, I began talking to her, trying to playfully convince her that I was a good guy to be trusted. Coincidence or not, soon after that she changed: she still froze if anyone else placed her hand on her mom's belly, but she now happily kept kicking if my hand was there.

So, figuring she had nothing to lose and that perhaps the coincidences would continue, Elizabeth talked to Isabella. "We have the birthing pool set up and everything is ready for you now. If you are ready, I'd love for you to come now."

It was shortly before midnight on July 1, and soon after the "talk" we fell asleep. A little over three hours later, Elizabeth woke me up. Labor had begun.

The whole experience was rather surreal. I had agreed to having Isabella at home because I trusted Elizabeth's medical expertise, and her confidence and understanding of her own body. But I was more than a bit freaked out. I was trying not to show it, but I was. After all, every single movie I had ever seen showing a woman giving birth had imprinted in my head a fairly horrific view of the whole thing, made of women screaming at the top of their lungs in agonizing pain. But if she wasn't scared, then to hell with my fears . . . What right did I have to be afraid? The least I could do for her was to keep my head together for this. Pleasantly, I found out that the movies were bullshit, or at least they were in our case. Elizabeth weathered the contractions simply by breathing heavily, as if she were in the midst of an intense yoga routine. In some ways it wasn't an easy labor, since for almost the entire time her contractions were coming on back-to-back with intervals that were much shorter than what medical manuals report as typical. But she dealt with them like a pro.

Eventually, the midwife arrived in the morning and helped Elizabeth move into a birthing pool we had set up in the living room. And it wasn't long after that that I stared into my daughter's eyes for the first time. Most babies born in a hospital are quite groggy, squint their eyes, and look very sleepy. Part of it may have to do with the fact that they have been pumped full of drugs as a result of the epidural given to the mother. Isabella surprised the hell out of me since she had big, open, alert eyes betraying a high level of awareness of her surroundings. Despite seeing me and two midwives around her, she needed no time to figure out which one was her mom, and promptly made clear that she wanted to be in her arms. After a suitable interval, I cut the umbilical cord and enjoyed my turn holding her.

And this is where my notoriously verbose self takes a bow and retires, because there truly are no words to describe the emotions that swept through me as I sat down holding my daughter for the first time.

CHAPTER 28

Heaven and Hell

We had fought tooth and nail every step of the way to be where we were. On paper everything looked great: Elizabeth had pulled becoming a doctor out of the magic hat, we had a beautiful daughter, I had built for myself a good niche teaching college and writing, we had bought a house. But as Hendrix sings, it was a castle made of sand.

Now that we were where we wanted, everything began crumbling down. Well, not everything—Iz was a dream, and we both adored her. Elizabeth was constantly exhausted, though. During pregnancy and shortly afterwards she wasn't able to work out like a savage the way she normally did to relieve stress. By now she was quicker to anger than she had ever been. Hardly anything made her happy. The journey had left deep scars. She had spent every ounce of energy to get here, but now had no gas left in the tank to enjoy it. And the overdose of years of frustration and low energy brought back the childhood demons she had been able to keep at bay in formerly strong times. Unresolved rage that had been buried away somewhere, seemingly safe, had broken out of its cage, and was now back with a vengeance.

In the midst of all of this, somehow she still managed to be super patient, loving, and wonderful to Isabella. Plenty of parents take out their problems on their kids, particularly when they cry for the thirtieth time at 3 AM as newborns invariably do. Not Elizabeth. Despite both of us going on virtually no sleep for the first few weeks, she kept her anger safely away from Isabella. She'd offer a never-ending source of love and sweetness to her . . . and was a fury to everyone else.

Under normal conditions, "everyone else" meant everyone but me, but these were not normal conditions. It is not exactly surprising that under the current monumental amount of accumulated stress we ended up fighting worse than ever. Apply enough pressure in somebody's life, start taking away sleep, leave the nerves exposed for too long, and everyone cracks. Tougher people can take much more pressure, sleep less, and yet endure longer than most. But in the end, it's all relative. Math and physics are unforgiving. Eventually, given enough weight on their shoulders, everything and everyone breaks.

The specifics of our fight may have seemed silly—most fights seem silly from a purely rational perspective. I wanted my father to fly from Italy to stay with us for a week and meet Isabella by the time she would be a couple of months old. Elizabeth wanted no one around. As a compromise, she accepted that he could stay for four days, but not an hour more. I felt it was complete and utter bullshit . . . my father flies across the *ocean* to meet his granddaughter and I have to show him the door after four days? Jesus Christ . . .

In her mind, she had made a huge compromise, and I was an ungrateful asshole. At such a delicate juncture, I should have had her back unquestioningly, and supported her 100 percent. Her home was her sanctuary and her safe place . . . why was I bringing anyone else into it? At a time when her stress level was off the charts, the last thing she needed was for me to argue with her.

Her logic was flawless, except that the picture looked quite different from where I stood.

Not arguing with her was easy if I were to let her have her way in every aspect of our lives. And for the most part I did. I had understood her need to be in control since the beginning of our relationship. But precisely because I already accommodated her in every way I could, I figured she could cut me some slack when I really needed her to give an inch. I didn't ask for much—ever. I just wanted to be comfortable having my father visit me in my own damn house for a few days.

It'd be easy to blame post-pregnancy hormones for the whole thing. It'd also be easy to blame the fact that the entire relationship was built on an uneven balance. My stupid notion that if I only tried hard enough, I could make everything ok, was not exactly working wonders for me at the moment. Regardless of the many possible factors at play here, the end result was the same. She wasn't so sure she could still trust me, and I felt like I gave everything I had to give only to find out it wasn't enough.

As it often happens with fights, the edges of this fight were dulled in time. In the weeks and months to come, we had plenty of tender, sweet moments that felt like old times. This, however, didn't take away the feeling that something there was badly strained. And it was yet to be seen whether it could be fully mended. I loved her and she loved me—we knew that much. Only time would tell if that would be enough.

CHAPTER 29

The Moments That Can Crush Your Soul

Had I known what was in store for us, the arguments we were having—that I thought were such a big deal at the time they were happening—would have appeared as child's play. A few months later I would have paid in gold to go back to the days when miscommunication and differing priorities were our biggest problems.

Our own personal hell didn't arrive amidst thunder and lightning. No parting of the sky. No riders of the apocalypse coming to announce the end. Nothing earth shattering. The beginning of the whole thing was so seemingly trivial that we didn't even know that the knock at our door was Hell asking to come in.

At the very end of the summer when our daughter turned one year old, Elizabeth woke with a very sore shoulder. That's it. I'm not kidding. Something as mundane as a stupid sore shoulder was literally the opening bell announcing that an ocean of pain was on its way.

The sore shoulder behaved as it is legitimate to expect a sore shoulder to behave—annoying, even painful, but nothing overly dramatic. We would talk about it for maybe a minute per day, and that was it. The only unusual characteristic was its stubborn persistence about being part of Elizabeth's life. It simply gave no sign of diminishing in intensity with the passing of time. "All that lifting up the baby and holding her constantly must have strained tendons and ligaments in there," rationalized Elizabeth. "And I'm sure the lack of sleep doesn't help either." Based on her words, I filed it under the "troublesome, but not alarming" category.

And yet not only did the little bastard not let up, but it got progressively worse. The status of her arm was becoming a serious damper on her overall mood. None of this improved when an orthopedic visit told her that there was nothing structurally wrong with the arm. No tear, no strain, no problems with ligaments, tendons, or muscles. Good news then? Not really, since it meant the source of the problem was to be found somewhere else.

If the orthopedic exam was the first warning, a much darker warning visited Elizabeth just a few days later, during a walk. The same type of pain and soreness now extended to her leg on the same side of the body as the injured shoulder. For the first time, her eyes flashed with some real concern. "What the hell is happening to my body?" she asked me—simultaneously knowing that I didn't have the answer and worrying about what the correct answer may be.

By the end of October, I had Isabella strapped to me as I was walking up and down the corridors of a neurologist's office where Elizabeth was getting checked out. If the good doctor had ever played poker, he clearly had forgotten all about it: his face gave away he was not having happy thoughts. The preliminary neurological exams clearly showed something was way off.

Her finger waved uncontrollably as she tried to touch objects in front of her nose.

Shit.

Fear had now made its way into our house and wasn't about to leave anytime soon.

Most motivational speakers and self-help books attempting to teach people how to defeat their fears love to hammer on the concept that fear is unwarranted. They repeat over and over how fear is an overblown knee-jerk response to situations that are really not that bad. Their idea is that there's really nothing to fear because things in reality are not as scary as we paint them in our imagination. This is probably good advice for the all-too-common cases of people indulging in groundless phobias, but leaves you completely unprepared to deal with the heavy stuff. What if reality turns out just as bad as the worst-case scenario you could imagine? Then what? We were about to find out.

The next stop in our descent into hell arrived barely two months after the initial shoulder pain. After a barrage of exams, the neurologist had an answer for us: Elizabeth had visible lesions in her brain consistent with multiple sclerosis.

Bad news—no question about it. But it could have been worse. By now, Elizabeth could hardly move her arm and had difficulties walking. But the neurologist suggested that this was due to a particularly heavy attack of MS, and that things would improve dramatically once the attack was over. Many people manage to live for a long time coexisting with their MS, so as unwelcome of a diagnosis as this was, it was no death sentence.

If nothing else it gave us something to hang on to—at least a promise that things may get much better as we learned to manage her condition. And we needed that vague sense of hope as much as we needed oxygen, for we were drowning. Her physical decline had been brutally rapid and there was still no end in sight. By November she had been in and out of the hospital multiple times, had to quit her job, and was walking with a cane. It was getting impossible for her to take care of Isabella, and even difficult to take care of herself. So I dug deep and pushed harder to keep things going, taking care of both of them.

As difficult as handling all finances and daily practical issues for all of us was, it was nothing compared to how painful it was to deal with the emotional aspect of it all. Try this, for example. At the end of another exhausting day burning the candle from every conceivable end, I joined her in bed so we could catch at least a few hours of sleep. But tears were flowing freely out of her eyes. As I hugged her close to me, she let out two words that broke my heart: "Why me?"

I looked at her and saw more vulnerability in her face than I had ever seen in the twelve years we had been together.

"I'm a good person," she insisted between the tears, "why is this happening to me?"

I'm sure I had been hurt worse other times in my life, but I sure as hell couldn't remember when. Her words . . . the expression on her face . . . the feeling of absolute powerlessness we shared . . . they all crushed my soul.

"You are a good person," I wanted to tell her, "and there is no why. Sometimes there is no rhyme or reason. Sometimes the universe is just fucked-up."

But I kept my cheerful existential thoughts to myself, hugged her tight, and voiced my belief that somehow, against all logic, we were going to come out all right from the nightmare we were in.

On another November night, the same conversation was playing on repeat. I kept telling her I firmly believed it was just a matter of time before the attack would subside, and we were going to figure out a way to manage her MS.

"What if it doesn't get better?" she asked me point blank.

"You will get better," I replied. "You just will."

"Why? What makes you think so?"

"Because . . ." The lack of any encouraging evidence wasn't going to stop my sentence. "Because we are supposed to go grocery shopping together when we are eighty."

This was a running topic of conversation that we had kept up for years. It had started one day early in our relationship, when I told her I was looking forward to growing old with her, and was excited at the thought of the two of us still going grocery shopping hand in hand when we would be eighty years old. That image—us, old and grey, holding each other as we picked groceries after a life spent together—would show up often in our chats. And right now, even though I had nothing rational to offer to support my belief that everything was going to be ok, I wasn't letting go of that image. If nothing else, it made her smile. The smile, however, wasn't altering the trajectory of her thoughts.

"I'm tired, baby," she said with detached calm. "I can't do this much longer."

Just in case the message wasn't explicit enough, she spelled out that she wanted to kill herself.

This was no idle desperate cry for attention. She wanted the highest quality of life or she would rather not live at all. She had made this point abundantly clear ever since I had known her. This was one of the bedrocks of her philosophy of life. She brought this up many times a year for every year I had been with her. She was utterly unafraid of death. The only thing scaring her was the thought of being forced to live in a dramatically diminished capacity.

"I never want to slowly waste away," she said with unfailing regularity. "I want to live life on my terms or be done with it.

Promise me you never let me lose myself a piece at a time. Promise you don't guilt-trip me into staying alive at all costs."

And then she'd run through all the possible scenarios in which she was incapacitated and it was up to me to choose to pull the plug or keep her alive, or similar morbid thoughts. Typically, she wouldn't let up until I promised. Only then would she calm down, and we could go back to enjoying whatever we were doing.

But in this case, I didn't feel like I was going back on my promise.

"You are just exhausted, my love," I protested. "You have been through absolute hell for three months now. Of course, you feel like giving up. But things are going to get better. I'm not asking you to stick around if your quality of life remains what it is now. Things will be better and this will just seem like a bad dream. Just hold on a bit longer."

"You really believe it?"

"I do, or I wouldn't be encouraging you."

"How long?"

Like I fucking know . . . "Give yourself a chance. I tell you what . . . if by summer you are not all better, I'll go looking for a baseball bat and finish you off myself."

Horrendously dark humor always made her laugh. It did this time too. And more importantly, it convinced her to push suicide to the back burner. The way she saw things, this was a fair deal she could live with. I wasn't trying to convince her to stay alive no matter how horrible her quality of life. I was just asking for a chance to let us figure out a way out of the MS attack from hell.

And yet, the days and weeks to come didn't offer even a glimpse of any encouraging sign. On the contrary, her physical condition kept deteriorating at record speed. Her arm had turn to jelly and rested inert against her body. She couldn't lift it or move it in any way. I remember how one day the two of us were giving Isabella a bath. I was singing a song for Iz and she showed her approval by clapping her tiny hands together. Something was odd, though ... She wasn't clapping with both hands. Instead she had placed a hand in her lap and was using the other to clap against it—an all too obvious attempt to imitate the way she had seen her mother clap now that she could only move one arm. In another of the many soul-crushing things that seemed to fill our days, I saw Elizabeth's smile die on her face. Her daughter was learning movement from her mom—as is natural—but those were the movements of an invalid. Just a few months earlier, Elizabeth had been in top athletic shape. Now she couldn't even clap—something awful for anyone to deal with, but for someone as strong and fiercely independent as Elizabeth, it was pure hell.

And one of her legs seemed to be about to follow on the same path. By December I had to carry her in my arms to bring her up and down the stairs to and from our bedroom. A few times, she fell while trying to go to the bathroom on her own. And Isabella, who had barely learned how to walk herself, would scream "Mama!" and rush to try to pick her up. Soul-crushing moments piling on top of more soul-crushing moments. Pure rage in Elizabeth's eyes as she saw herself descending into increasing levels of powerlessness—her physical body basically giving up on her.

In all of this, I more or less had to quit sleeping. During the day, I was either working or taking care of Isabella. During the night, I would take care of Elizabeth: she could hardly sleep and her mind would run in circles, torturing her, not to mention the help she needed getting to the bathroom. I was running like a madman morning through night through morning, trying to put a finger in every hole in the dam. I pushed every fiber of my being trying to save all that I loved only to see it collapse all around me.

In one of our all-night conversations, she told me how sad she was about the prospect of being alone, about being removed from Isabella and me. I thought she was talking about her visits to the hospital, so I reassured her that those were only temporary. We'd always be with her. We'd never leave her. When she clarified her meaning, I felt like a cannonball hit me. She wasn't talking about the hospital. She was afraid that death would take her away from us and she would no longer be close to her daughter and me . . . There was absolutely nothing I could say or do to comfort her or chase away that feeling. The only way would have been to blatantly lie, but neither one of us was in the habit of lying to ourselves or to each other out of fear.

CHAPTER 30

"We Are Born into a World in Which No Quarter Is Given"

I'm no medical expert, but even I can understand that, as a general rule, it's not a good thing when a doctor comes to report the results of your latest MRI with quivering lip and tears in her eyes.

It was January. Less than five months from when Elizabeth's shoulder pain had initially showed up. And we were back in the emergency room yet again, after another dramatic worsening of the symptoms.

When the doctor finally found the strength to speak, the news she brought mirrored her facial expression. The lesions in the brain had more than doubled in size in the few weeks since the last MRI. It turns out that the MS diagnosis had been wrong. Only a biopsy could tell us for sure what we were dealing with, but it was almost certain it was a brain tumor. And it looked like it was a particularly aggressive type, moving at killer speed. Before we even had a chance to absorb the blow and process it all, the doc continued. She wasn't quite done with the bad news. The location of the tumor in the brain was particularly unfortunate, since any surgery in that area would leave Elizabeth in a vegetative state. In other words, it wasn't just a brain tumor. It wasn't just a super aggressive form that had likely progressed to an advanced stage already. But it was also inoperable. It was going to kill Elizabeth. The only question was how long it would take.

The doc tried to put a semi-smile on her face, suggesting that she had heard of miraculous cases when people in her condition could last two or three years, and that maybe Elizabeth's case could be one of those. If that was her idea of delivering good news, she sucked at it. Two or three years in the condition she was in? That's when I knew.

Elizabeth was not going to sit around waiting for a "miracle," since the doc's idea of a miracle was Elizabeth's idea of hell.

Some people in her situation would try to hold on in any possible way, milking every extra day they could stay alive. Some would rationalize that they were doing it to be close to their children. Elizabeth, clearly, was not one of those people. Based on everything I knew about her, I was sure that prolonging the agony she was experiencing while bringing a heavy wave of sadness into her baby's life was not on her to-do list.

A few minutes after taking in what couldn't be described as anything but a death sentence, she responded like the freakishly fearless person that she was. For the past few months, she had been on a super strict diet designed to help her fight the symptoms of MS. Except that it wasn't MS after all. So, her first comment about her terminal brain tumor was, "When we get out of here, take me to eat all the tastiest, most fattening, least healthy foods out there. Everything I haven't eaten lately, I want." I gave her the warmest smile I could muster and signed up to be her accomplice in this defiant plan, "Consider it done, baby. What-ever you want ... just name it."

But we weren't going to be home anytime soon. First, they would admit her to intensive care, carve her head open, and go digging around her brain. The hospital was going to be our home for a while. I brought Isabella to stay with my mom so I could sleep next to Elizabeth. Ok ... maybe "sleep" is an overly optimistic assessment of the situation. One of the side effects of the brain tumor was that she had been largely unable to keep her eyes closed for more than three hours per night, even while downing sleeping pills that could knock out a bull. So, sleep was not on the menu for me either, but at least I could spend the night next to her, holding her, talking to her, kissing her, helping her to and from the bathroom.

During one of these never-ending days/nights (under the fluorescent hospital lights it was difficult to tell the difference), I saw the patient tag on her wrist: "Han, Elizabeth. Female. Age: 36." That's when the realization sunk in that there was a very high chance she wouldn't live to see her 37th birthday. Up until that moment, the trajectory of her life had looked like a poster for the American Dream: the child of illegal immigrants, raised in the midst of poverty and abuse, she had clawed her way out of misery to become a doctor, have a baby, marry someone she loved, and carve for herself some happiness . . . a true success story of overcoming crazy odds . . . except that there would not be any happy ending at the end of the rainbow. No damn American Dream. Just random death and meaningless tragedy.

Ancient Roman philosopher Seneca had it right. We truly are "born into a world in which no quarter is given." Life is deaf to our pleas. Whatever sentimental notion I may have held about living in a universe governed by some sort of justice and fairness evaporated before my eyes.

She didn't verbalize it much, and didn't like to dwell on it, but she was perfectly aware that this was it for her. We were having a visit in the hospital with our friend Marlon Mercado—a man who was like a brother to her—and were talking about working out, something we all enjoyed tremendously. I was whining about the sorry state of my physical shape. It was the first time in twenty years that I hadn't trained like a savage for an extended period of time, and I was getting edgy about it. Elizabeth just gave me a big smile and said, "Don't worry, baby. You'll get there again."

The second the words came out of her lips I felt an unbearable pain. Just how stupid was I to dare complain about my own body considering what she was going through? But even more painful than being made aware of my stupidity was her saying nothing about her own future. She didn't say anything because she knew she had none. She knew her body was never going to regain its amazing shape. And she was clearly alluding to a future in which I'd get to go to the gym again, and she'd be no more.

Despite the presence of death never leaving the room, Elizabeth somehow stayed on course. The night before her biopsy she was up late shopping on amazon.com looking for a birthday gift for her nephew . . . such an ordinary activity in the midst of the most atrocious of times.

The procedure was brutally long. Her sister Belle and I were in the waiting area for hours after they told us she would be out—hours in which our whole lives were suspended; the verdict on our entire future hanging from the lips of the surgeon who had spent the day cutting her head open. By the time he came out to talk to us, it was clear that the doc was much more comfortable slicing brains with a knife than talking about his findings to other human beings. Not that I could blame him, considering the news he was bringing us. In an emotionless monotone, he told us he had cut through layers and layers of necrotic tissue. He had no doubts: it was a large tumor. The only question left was at what stage it was. Elizabeth's sister Belle pushed him to spill his thoughts in the way only a Han family member can push somebody. And so he told her we'd have to wait for the analysis of the tissue to be sure, but he was fairly sure it was a stage four—the deadliest diagnosis possible.

Even though I had expected that answer, I felt like my insides were ripped out of me. The tiny little sliver of hope that I had been hanging on to against all reason was squashed before my eyes. I felt something die inside of me, and emotionally everything went numb. In my worst nightmares, I had pictured that news like this would make me scream and rage. I had imagined my emotions would take over and tear me to pieces. Belle reacted exactly the way I had anticipated I'd react myself—sobbing uncontrollably, collapsing against the wall of the hallway, gasping for breath. The opposite was happening inside of me. I turned ice cold. In many ways, Belle's reaction pushed me in that direction. A part of me felt precisely like she did. I wanted to yell and punch walls, but the fact that she let it all out forced me to balance things by trying to be as pragmatic and stable as possible. My freaking out and losing it was not going to help Elizabeth when she would wake up. And right now, helping her in whatever way she needed was the only thing that mattered. She was dying, but she wasn't dead yet—which meant that she'd need my energy more than ever before now.

In that instant, my whole focus shifted. Up until that moment, I had been hurting and suffering and praying and hoping . . . but once all hope was yanked away from me, something in me snapped. In the weeks to come, I'd be by her side constantly—day and night. I had one job and one job only, and that was to make her smile. My own emotions were swept aside because . . .

well, because I wasn't the one fucking dying. They'd only take up energy and focus that I badly needed to direct to her.

I'd leave her side for maybe an hour a day to go take a shower at my mom's house. The second I'd leave her room, I'd crumble to pieces, and my repressed emotions would come back with a vengeance. They would hit me all of a sudden with renewed intensity. Breathing would be a struggle. I'd cry uncontrollably. Anybody taking a picture of me at the wheel, as I was driving the distance from the hospital to the house, would have seen a river of tears and a face frozen in a silent scream. Nothing anyone could say or do would make things a tiny bit better. It was hell. But it was hell on a timer. I didn't have the luxury to give in to my grief. Within an hour I would have to forcibly close the gates of hell and be back by her side. So, right before I went back in the room with her, I'd chase all the heartbreak away, put my game face on, and find a way to smile.

Don't get me wrong—I wasn't bullshitting her by offering her false hope or pretending everything was ok. It wasn't that kind of smile. Death was knocking at the door, and no amount of pretending otherwise was going to change that. I wasn't one to insult her intelligence, and she wasn't one to want it. The smile was about something else entirely. It was about finding something to be happy about for that one second we were sharing, and then for the second after that, and the one after that yet. When we laughed together, we'd turn her hospital bed into a place that fear, anxiety, and pain couldn't reach. There was no way I could soothe my own pain, but I could find the strength to do it for her. I was determined to give my utmost best for every minute we still had together. The future in store for us was made of nothing but tragedy. But this was no reason not to find a way to enjoy whatever time we had.

And so I spent days and nights running up and down the hospital, constantly on the prowl to make things more comfortable for her, doing whatever she needed, guarding the door in the rare moments when she'd fall asleep to make sure nurses wouldn't wake her.

Paradoxically, it was precisely at this juncture that every minute I had ever spent doing martial arts paid off for me. For many years, in training I had been pushing myself far out of my comfort zone. I had struggled with fighting on when every muscle in my body screamed at me to give up. I had worked through physical exhaustion, and wave after wave of self-defeating emotions. The game had been all about carrying on when physical and emotional obstacles tried to break me. Now, obviously anything I had ever done on the mat had been a joke compared to what we were experiencing. And yet it helped me to stay by Elizabeth's side with uncrushed spirit despite the fact that we both knew we were in a losing fight. Staying in a fight, perhaps even enjoying the fight, when you have no hope of victory . . . that was without a doubt the most important thing I had ever learned from combat sports.

Right now, we were going on no sleep, little food, and zero hope. I was seeing a person I adored being taken away from me inch by inch, and I was completely powerless to do anything about it. I wanted to bash my head against the wall. I wanted to escape the present situation. I wanted to avoid it in any way possible. But she couldn't escape it nor avoid it. And so, neither would I. All around us were overwhelming emotions threatening our sanity if we gave in to them. We were on a tightrope at the edge of the abyss. One inch in one direction, and we could fall prey to some self-delusional optimism and ridiculous hopes. This would shield us from pain for the present moment, but set us up for prolonged pain down the road once reality would knock us on our asses. One inch in the other direction, and we would be letting tragedy break us, leaving us open to an invasion of gloom and doom. Neither of these options offered us anything good. So . . . to hell with both. We were going to go down our own way, finding a way to laugh in the face of death.

In the midst of all this, it became obvious to her that whatever tension we may have had a few months prior was complete bullshit. She now knew again beyond any doubt that I loved her as much as any human being can love another, and I fully had her back. During one of our interminable, sleepless nights, she said so.

I told her, "I'd rather you hated me but you were healthy and happy rather than you loving me in these circumstances. But we don't get to have a voice in this, do we?"

She smiled at me and hugged me. "No, my love. We don't."

CHAPTER 31

The Death of a Queen

When a samurai is to commit *seppuku*, he will ask a friend to serve as a *kaishakunin*—a second in charge of helping him ease the agony of ritual suicide by beheading him when the pain from stabbing himself is about to overwhelm him.

From the moment when the doctor told us it'd be a miracle if Elizabeth survived longer than another month, I knew what awaited us. She wanted to be able to go on her own terms, without having to languish away one piece at a time, losing bits of her dignity and independence at every step.

"Bring me home," she told me after the latest night in the hospital. "Take me away from the tubes, and the needles, and the fluorescent lights. I don't want Isabella to visit me in a hospital. Let's go home."

She could barely keep her eyes open, but her smile brightened at the thought of returning to her house and smelling the lavender and the rosemary planted outside our windows.

She had already spelled out her wishes to me. She didn't want to die in a hospital among nurses and doctors. She wanted to go back to a place where she had known much happiness, where she had given birth to our daughter, where she felt as good as she could feel anywhere. She wanted to visit and share some laughter with friends and family for a few days. And then she'd die.

Her sisters were not too keen about this plan. The idea of Elizabeth being no more was something that they just couldn't bear. Belle, in particular, had a hard time accepting the death of loved ones. A few years earlier, during a visit, she had told us about a friend of hers battling a stage four tumor, and strongly voiced her belief that—despite the fairly grim medical prognosis—her friend would come through and be healed. Not wanting to upset her, Elizabeth hadn't contradicted her. Once we were alone though, she made it clear she thought her sister was in denial.

"Belle doesn't want to face it, but her friend is gone. In her friend's future are a few months of misery, pain, and treatments that will only keep the illusion going for a little longer. Belle tells herself she'll get through this because she can't deal with death, but the writing is on the wall. It's already over."

Time proved Elizabeth right, and things played out exactly the way she had predicted.

Not long after that, my aunt was struck with an aneurysm, fell into a coma, and was left with severe brain damage. My mother abandoned her life in the United States to race back to Italy and be close to her. For the next two years she stood nearly 24/7 by her side, holding on to the hope that she could bring her back. During this time, she wrecked her own health pouring every ounce of energy into achieving the impossible. After what seemed like an endless amount of pain and suffering for her and her sister, she saw there was no way out, and had to let her go.

On both occasions, with what in hindsight would look like an eerie prophetic clarity, Elizabeth sat me down, looked into my eyes with the intensity only she could muster, and said,

"Never, ever let me be in that place. Love may blind you to think that you have to push me in every way to stay alive. But if you really love me, you will let me go. I don't fear death. And I need you not to fear it either." So, for the zillionth time I promised her I would do as she wished.

But that was then—a hypothetical discussion about a future that would probably never materialize. Except that now that same hypothetical scenario was our reality.

Her family didn't understand how she felt. It wasn't their fault. Despite how much she loved her sisters, Elizabeth had chosen that the "what to do if I'm close to death" speech would not be part of their monthly conversations. She had saved that for our talks. Yeah . . . lucky me.

Not surprisingly, her family kept pushing her toward all sorts of invasive procedures that were the exact opposite of what she wanted. She would feebly protest, but then couldn't bear the sadness in her sisters' eyes. And so she'd end up agreeing to their suggestions—not because she believed any of this could help her, but because she didn't want to be the one to yank their hopes away.

She was at peace with this change of direction, then? Not even close. The second her sisters went to sleep, she'd spend the rest of the night telling me how much she just wanted to be able to die in peace. The few moments at night when she would fall asleep, she always reverted to being a child, and would call out for her father in Chinese. Once she would wake, she would have no memory of any of this. But even after these weird interludes ended, frustration and rage would take over, and her rational side would take a leave until morning. One night, she was so bugged by the delays in removing the stitches left in her head from the biopsy that she thought it was a good idea to call a doctor friend of hers at 4 AM to come remove them. No amount of pleading to wait until morning and let her friend sleep prevailed.

The clash between what she told me and what she would tell her sisters drove me insane. Knowing how much she just wanted them to let her go, and then seeing her yielding to their plans for aggressive treatment, hurt me to the core. It was like watching someone being raped in front of me. But to be truthful, as much as I wanted to blame it on someone else, this was no one's fault but hers. Had she stuck to her guns, they would have had to accept it. The problem was that she cared too much for them, and she'd rather hurt herself than hurt them. Enough pushing, pleading, and badgering would regularly overcome her defenses.

Everyone's nerves were raw from exhaustion, fear, and mind-numbing sadness, so it didn't take much for tempers to flare. On a couple of occasions, I was so enraged by Belle's pushing Elizabeth in directions that were clearly the opposite of what she wanted that I got into some serious verbal battles with her. After days of this, we had settled on an uneasy compromise. Belle accepted Elizabeth's decision to return home to receive hospice care on the condition that she'd still agree to begin chemotherapy in a few days. The whole arrangement obviously made no sense since hospice care is for when you have basically accepted that death is inevitable, whereas chemo is not. Elizabeth had spent years in medical school telling me on a regular basis how she'd much rather die than go through chemo, so I knew it wasn't going to happen. But for the time being, the compromise was what allowed us to return home without further drama. There was a mandatory wait between the biopsy and chemo, so the next round of battle could wait for a while.

In the meantime, just because I wasn't feeling enough pressure already, the first visit with the hospice nurse ended with her taking me to a separate room, and asking me straight up, "Are you going to be the one to do what she needs to be done?"

Considering that the legal status of euthanasia is akin to murder, the nurse was tiptoeing with her words, but wasn't too subtle either.

"What 'needs to be done,'" I replied, "is whatever Elizabeth wants. If she wants help going, I'll help her go. If she wants help staying, I'll help her stay."

I already had too many voices in my head. I really didn't care what any of them thought was the best course of action. There was only one voice that mattered. And it was Elizabeth's. Everything else was background noise.

Despite decisions about life and death looming on the horizon, something else managed to catch my attention. Facing death was making Elizabeth's personality change at an amazing speed.

"I feel so lucky," she told me the day we left the hospital.

"Come again?"

"Well . . . other than the deadly tumor in my brain I mean," she laughed.

My face turned into a question mark.

"I never realized I have so many people in my life who love me and are so good to me."

Ever since I had known her, a sense of deep loneliness had stalked Elizabeth. She had the same high standards about friendship that she had about everything else and was unwilling to make compromises about them. The result was that she had very few friends—and even saying "few" was being generous. But now, in her moment of deepest vulnerability, her defenses vanished, and she was free to appreciate every kind gesture. It was as if she had become aware of people's love for her for the first time. Over and over I saw her having deep, heartfelt connections with the friends visiting her at the hospital and after we returned home. It was beautiful to watch. Her typical distrust and anger had given way to unbounded kindness. She was able to give and receive love in a way that had been impossible only weeks earlier.

One of her visitors was a doctor named José Camacho, whose practice she had joined a few months earlier. They talked much about death, life, the universe, and everything else. A few hours after he left, I noticed she was unusually upset. Not because the visit had been unpleasant. Quite the contrary, actually.

"I was in the perfect frame of mind to die," she said. "No fear. No worries. I'm mad I missed this chance."

The perfect frame of mind to die . . . I can't even begin to imagine what she was going through. As brave as she was, the awareness that in a few days or weeks she'd be no more must have been overwhelming. I had heard some people voice the opinion that death is harder for those who stay behind to become the prisoners of grief than for those actually dying . . . Utter and complete bullshit. As horrible as I was feeling, I wasn't the one seeing my body melting away; I wasn't the one having to abandon everything I held dear; and I wasn't the one looking at my infant daughter knowing I'd never be there to see her grow up.

As tough and iron-willed as she was, she wasn't immune to moments of weakness. Only once since we had come back home had I seen her allowing herself a rare chance to vent. Tears streamed down her face—her body slightly trembling with a mix of sadness and anger.

"I am mad about being given so little time with her," she managed to say while crying, speaking of Isabella.

But she quickly caught herself. It's almost as if she knew that opening that emotional door was going to make everything much more painful. Raging at the injustices of life wasn't going to help her. And so, just as suddenly as she had opened that door, she slammed it back shut. She forced the tears back, chased away those thoughts, and steeled herself, trying to muster up the spirit she needed to get ready to die. A warrior if I ever saw one.

"I'd like to have Buddhist monks to see me on my way," she voiced shortly thereafter.

Elizabeth wasn't formally Buddhist, nor religious in a more generic sense, so I had no clue where the request was coming from. I also had no idea what exactly she wanted from the Buddhist monks, and wasn't sure she knew either. But it didn't matter. I didn't need to know how or why. My job was to help her in any way she needed, so out the door I went, hunting for Buddhist monks.

As luck would have it, there was a Tibetan Buddhist temple just a few blocks from our home. Even though I wasn't too clear about what the hell I was doing there or what I was asking for, the people at the temple seemed to understand the purpose of my visit better than I did. The second I started telling our story, they bent over backwards trying to facilitate things for us. They were insanely kind, and in no time set things in motion to address Elizabeth's request, even to the point of dragging the head of the temple, Geshe Lobsang Tsultrim, away from a meeting so he could talk to me. Despite his heavy Tibetan accent and my heavy Italian accent, we understood each other perfectly. If his religion had anything to do with his personality, Buddhism was winning some points in my eyes. He dropped everything he was doing and sent for some fellow monks, so they could walk to our house immediately. One of the guys he wanted was nowhere to be found, and he apparently was an important part of whatever they were planning, but Lobsang had a good hunch of where to find him.

"There's a Starbucks on the way to your house. I'm sure we'll find him there. He really loves his Starbucks." Sure enough, once Lobsang got a hold of him on the phone, the lost monk arrived running, out of breath and still clutching a cup of coffee in his hands. If the context hadn't been so damn heavy, the whole thing would have been funny. And so we returned home: me leading the way followed by five or six Tibetan monks in traditional robes plus Starbucks coffee . . .

They all sat on the floor close to Elizabeth's bed, and began to chant for her. There was something haunting and beautiful about their singing. Neither Elizabeth nor I understood any of the theological significance of what was going on, but this was not about understanding. The chanting was touching deep emotional chords that entirely bypassed rational understanding. It was primal. It was powerful. And apparently it was exactly what Elizabeth needed, since she relaxed like I hadn't seen her relax in weeks, and fell asleep in the midst of the ceremony.

"Call me again," Lobsang said, "when she is about to pass. We'll come back and chant for her to help her through."

All the pieces Elizabeth wanted were beginning to fall into place. I somehow managed to track down her yoga teacher. Initially, since he had hundreds of regular students and hadn't seen her in almost a year, he hadn't understood who the Elizabeth I was talking about was, but once he did, he freed up his schedule for us and drove fifty miles to come see her.

As he said, "Had you told me from the get-go that we were talking about the Elizabeth who lights up the room when she smiles, I'd have known right away."

They spent an hour chatting and laughing as if the fact that she was dying had no power over their conversation. I can never repay the debt to this man for helping Elizabeth in that moment. Nor can I ever repay the debt of gratitude I owe to José Camacho and to her friends who came to visit her and showered her with love. This is something I can never forget.

But eventually the time to play was over. Her chemo appointment was coming up and she had to make a decision. At 3 AM, during yet another sleepless night, she asked me to pick up my video camera and record what she had to say. In one of the most painful moments of my life, I taped the message she wanted to deliver to her sisters. Years later, when I thought I was strong enough to watch the video again, I ended up crying for days. Her voice barely more than a whisper, she finally stated clearly that she just wished they could let her go. When she talked to them the next morning, she repeated the same.

"Dying," she told them, "is not what I am scared of."

"What is it then that scares you?" they asked

"The only thing I am afraid of is disappointing you. I am afraid you'll be mad at me for choosing the path I want."

And that's when everything changed. Whatever her sisters thought and wanted until a second earlier melted away. As tears flowed freely from many eyes, everyone rushed to reassure Elizabeth of their love and agreed to support whatever she wanted.

I was sure she'd now ask me to help her go. After all, that's what she had asked me to promise in hypothetical scenarios many, many times before.

But she didn't.

"Here's what's going to happen," she told me instead. "You are going to give me morphine for pain only in the amounts suggested by the doctor. Not a fraction more, not a fraction less. When they allow you to increase the amounts, great. But let's stick exactly to what they say."

Hospice care allows the use of morphine—even in relatively heavy amounts—to help terminal patients cope with pain. What no one ever discusses is that strong doses of morphine also speed up the dying process. The hypocrisy of the law about this is infuriating. Euthanasia is not allowed, so you can give increasing amounts of morphine that will contribute to someone's death in a matter of hours, or possibly days, but you can't give someone a big shot of morphine all at once that allows a patient to die painlessly in a matter of minutes. We do the latter for our pets, but somehow can't extend the same courtesy to our loved ones among humans. Religious notions about "only God decides when a life ends" are still prevalent enough as to be law. I have no problem whatsoever with people choosing to hold on to life to the bitter end. It's their body. It's their life. And no one else should choose for them. What I have serious problems with is when these people can't return the favor and allow other people to choose how they want to die. The imposition of someone's set of moral priorities on everyone else is pure fascism in my eyes. And the idea that now my lady had to think about these kinds of issues at the moment she was facing death enraged me. Let the woman deal with the most dramatic experience anyone can deal with however she wants. Any law that interferes with this is a totalitarian perversion.

"This is not what you have always asked me to do."

I simply wasn't catching on. Legal considerations were so far from my mind that they didn't even enter the picture.

"It's not really what I want now either," she tried to explain. "But anti-euthanasia laws being what they are, doing what I want would put you on a collision course with the law."

"I don't give a fuck about the law. I only care about giving you what you want and need."

She smiled and kissed me, "And this is part of why I love you, but I don't want you to do anything that can land you in jail."

"I don't give a fuck about jail either. If my helping you go the way you want lands me in jail, so be it."

"Isabella will no longer have her mom. Think about it. It's a heavy thing for such a little one. She can't be missing her dad too."

Fuck . . . I took one look at Isabella and knew immediately that Elizabeth was right. I wanted to punch a wall. I wanted to rip apart some self-righteous moralist willing to sacrifice other people's freedom on the altar of his own brand of morality. I was fuming. Everything was already so damn heartbreaking, and to top it all off my lady was even denied the right to die how she wanted. There are no words in the English language to describe how angry I was.

And yet I was also filled with love—love for Elizabeth. Here she was, knocking at Death's door, at a time when it'd have been legitimate for her to be concerned only with herself, and yet she was thinking about Isabella's welfare and mine.

Ok, then. If she wasn't going to let it bother her, neither would I. We'd do things by the book, and stick to the closest thing to what she wanted that was legally allowed.

Given the terrible physical condition she was in, the hospice doctor had no hesitation authorizing increasing amounts of morphine for her. Her body was clearly reaching the end of the ride.

And so it began.

Once she decided to start the morphine, there were no second thoughts. She didn't ask to see Isabella. She didn't indulge in melodramatic speeches or tearful goodbyes. She had hit her stride, and wanted nothing to take her focus away. The time for words was over. No hesitation. No regrets. She was a warrior on a mission.

By nature, I'm freakishly sensitive and highly emotional. And there really was no moment in my life that should have been as emotionally charged as this. But everything in me went ice cold. I saw nothing and felt nothing other than what was needed to be there for her. Both Elizabeth and martial arts had taught me to cut the bullshit and be in the moment. In martial arts, everything you were and everything you will be mean nothing. The only thing that matters is what you can muster in those few seconds or minutes in the ring or on the mat—give 100 percent here and now so that you'll have nothing to regret later, regardless of the outcome. Whining about the past or wondering about the future are equally useless, and even dangerous since another punch is flying in the air in this very moment aimed for your head. Whatever martial arts had taught me, Elizabeth had reinforced. She never regretted anything about her past. The way she explained it, "I wouldn't be who I am here and now if things didn't happen the way they did. I like who I am, so I'm not going to give space in my life to regrets or useless speculation."

In the present situation, neither one of us ever went down the "had we caught this earlier" path. We refused to waste time and energy wondering what might have been. It probably wouldn't have made a difference anyway. And even if it would have . . . nothing we could do about it now.

Almost thirteen years of a relationship together and it came down to this . . . me feeding her morphine around the clock, her life slowly ebbing away as we held hands. The whole scene looked eerily ordinary. She lay in bed with her eyes closed. Her sisters and I were right next to her. A soundtrack she had requested played in the background around the clock—beautiful music that I'll never be able to listen to again. In the next room, our daughter napped peacefully. When at some point Elizabeth woke up, the only thing she wanted to know was if Isabella was ok. Once she was reassured that she was, she went back to sleep.

Per the doctor's instructions, we were supposed to give her drops of liquid morphine under her tongue around the clock. The few moments when I fell asleep next to her in the middle of the night, something in me would wake me up almost exactly fifty-nine minutes later—as if my body was running by some sort of internal clock. The day faded into night and faded into day again. After a while, I no longer had any idea what day it was, but my body somehow kept track of the hour-long cycle Elizabeth was on.

Eventually, my mom took our daughter to her house. She didn't really need to be around for the last hours when inevitably heavy emotions would fill the air. Both her sisters were by her bedside every step of the way. The whole experience would break their hearts in the months to come, but in that moment they demonstrated the bravery and strength that Elizabeth needed. Sumati, a friend of ours who had been Elizabeth's classmate in medical school, came to support us—an act of touching generosity and toughness, since I can't imagine this was either pleasant or easy for her. The whole process was brutal. Morphine's side effects can cause somebody to choke on their own saliva, and other painful reactions, so we had to constantly be ready to give her other medicines to make sure she wouldn't experience any discomfort.

As promised, the Tibetan monks came back to chant for her when it became clear that she had started the journey, and that she wasn't going to wake up again. And even then . . . nothing was quick or easy. Many times, she took a deep breath and didn't exhale. We'd all look at each other, and just when we thought that maybe it was over she'd breathe again.

At one point, Belle asked Sumati how much time Elizabeth had left ahead of her. Sumati told her it'd be at least a few more hours, so Belle took leave to go to the bathroom. This was the first time since the whole thing had started that neither of her sisters was in the room with us. Almost as if on cue, my lady took her last breath right there and then, as I was holding her hand. To the very end, she was unafraid and ready to go.

CHAPTER 32

The Smile

Geshe Lobsang Tsultrim had given me precise instructions for the time of her death.

"Once she stops breathing, no one should touch her. Don't cry in front of her. If you have to, leave the room. When someone stops breathing, their spirit will be trying to leave the body. Touching them and crying in front of them is going to make them want to stay close to you. And this makes things more difficult for them. Try to leave them alone for at least a couple of hours."

Once Sumati confirmed Elizabeth was gone, for a second my eyes filled up with tears. But I promptly wiped them away and kicked everyone out of the room. I had no idea if the Tibetan monks were right or if they were full of it, but I wasn't going to take chances. My feelings were kept on hold. I heard desperate crying from those who had stepped out of the house, but I wasn't ready to give my emotions free rein. As far as I knew, I was still a man on a mission—my determination to make sure she could go in the best possible way didn't end when her breathing stopped.

Two hours later, we were back by her side. Since she was no longer struggling, her face had relaxed, but there was nothing too unusual about it. She simply looked as if she was napping. It was good to see her face finally free from pain.

For another hour or two, we kept going back to her—to steal another glance, knowing full well that these were the last occasions when we'd ever get to lay eyes on her.

But again, nothing unusual about her face.

It was a full six hours later when things got strange. I went into the room for one more visit with my lady, and that's when I noticed it. Elizabeth had the biggest smile on her face—a smile that hadn't shown up when she died, or an hour later, or two, or three. But now it was there—unmistakable. Her sisters walked in the room after me, and they immediately looked at each other.

"Do you see it too?"

"I see it . . . she . . . she is smiling!"

"What's going on? How can she be smiling?"

None of us had any idea. It's one thing for the facial muscles to relax upon death. It's a whole other thing to flash a blissful smile six hours after the fact.

In case things weren't weird enough, they were about to get weirder. Since I never wanted to forget this image, I reached for the camera and decided to take a picture. I brought the camera to my eyes and . . . as I looked through the lens, the smile was no longer there. I lowered the camera, and the smile was still obviously there. I looked through the lens one more time, and again the smile had vanished. I played this game six or seven times. Each time I'd look through the lens, I could see no smile. But each time I looked at her directly, her smile was impossible to miss. I asked others to repeat my experiment, and the result was the same for everyone. The mouth of each new person who walked in the room inevitably opened wide. No one had told them anything to avoid influencing them, but we were all seeing the same thing.

Elizabeth was smiling.

Many people would react to this rushing to find an explanation. Some would try to explain it away through a purely materialistic model, and arguing that this was a particularly strange type of rigor mortis. Others would reach for detailed supernatural explanations. I don't know what made Elizabeth smile hours after she had stopped breathing, but I do know that it was beautiful. And it was the biggest gift she could have given me.

PART III

Answering
Hopelessness with
a Defiant Smile
and Raised
Middle Finger

CHAPTER 33

"Throw Me into Hell, and I'll Find a Way to Enjoy It"

The man at the mortuary acted the way you'd expect a man who spent his days dealing with death and grieving relatives to act: grave, somber, a bit stiff. The general sense of heaviness didn't lighten up when, after going over all the details, with a hint of embarrassment he passed me the bill for the cremation. Death was apparently an excellent business, since there were more digits on this bill than I could count. Not that I cared much at the moment—a high bill wasn't exactly the worst thing in my life those days. So, I opened my wallet and pulled out a quarter, and then a dime, and then another quarter while I began to count out loud the loose change I was digging out. As time passed and the coins began to pile up on the table, I could see a look of panic in the man's eyes, when he realized that I may be trying to pay him in quarters and dimes.

I let him sweat a little more before smiling at him, and saying, "I'm just fucking with you." I pulled out my checkbook and wrote him a check.

The mask of grave impenetrability broke and the man laughed his ass off.

"I don't get to laugh much in my line of work. Thank you."

What I discovered was that gallows humor was my survival strategy. I clung to it as a lifeboat and wielded it as a weapon. I didn't know how other people handled unbearable tragedy. Every moment since Elizabeth took her last breath had been a threat to my sanity. Just the night prior to my encounter with mortuary man, I had struggled going to sleep in the same bed where Elizabeth had died less than twenty-four hours earlier. I could still see her body lying there, her face on the pillow next to mine . . . If I dwelled even a tiny bit on the horror of it all, I could have never slept there again. And aside from the damn bed situation, if in a more general sense I dwelled on the horror of it all, I would have gone to pieces and no longer have been able to function.

This doesn't mean I was planning to be in denial and act as if everything was ok. The day I spoke at the memorial for Elizabeth I made this plenty clear. The speeches people normally give at memorials and funerals typically bug me. They usually try to exorcise horrific pain with trite formulas and sugarcoat the feeling of meaningless tragedy by rationalizing away those emotions. Either in its more traditional religious version: "It's God's will. Trust that He knows best. It's all part of His plan, and now our loved ones are in His presence." Or in the new age one: "Everything happens for a reason," these efforts to force meaning where meaning seems to be absent fail to console me.

Life is tough and people need all the help they can get dealing with it—I can appreciate that. If they need to embrace some cosmic, unseen, and unprovable explanation to somehow make sense of all their pain, and soften its bite, who the hell am I to tell them they shouldn't? I respect the fact that everyone needs to do what they have to do to get up in the morning, but I find this desire to avoid staring in the face at the ugly side of life a bit desperate and insincere.

Probably my "I am not going to bullshit you, myself, or Elizabeth by pretending I know she's in a better place or that everything works out for the best" opening wasn't the most traditional thing one might hear at a memorial. Neither was my mentioning that Elizabeth and I had likely made out on every one of the chairs where guests were sitting, since the memorial was taking place in a part of UCLA where we used to hang out when we first met. Elizabeth was brutally brave in facing both life and death. And I was going to honor her spirit by refusing to give in to comforting fairy tales or spineless rationalizations.

What I ended up saying was that Elizabeth was all about laughter—no matter what. She wasn't one to deny pain and suffering. But she definitely was one to find a way to smile and enjoy life in spite of them. In a similar spirit, my idol, Zen master Ikkyu Sojun, used to say, "Throw me into hell, and I'll find a way to enjoy it." We don't have a choice whether we end up on the gallows or not, but we do have a choice when it comes to having a sense of humor about it. The ability to laugh regardless of circumstances is the only weapon we have to face pain and tragedy. A broken heart and laughter can go hand in hand, after all.

Elizabeth, Ikkyu, and the universe had taught me something that I wasn't about to forget anytime soon: there's no escaping suffering, but this doesn't mean we have to let it have dominion over our lives either.

CHAPTER 34

How Do You Tell a Nineteen-Month-Old Baby That She'll Never See Her Mother Again?

The first time Isabella came back home with me after staying at my mother's house for a couple of days I realized I had a problem. Well . . . it was pretty clear I already had more than my share of problems, but it dawned on me that I had another one. Ever since she had learned how to walk, Isabella had religiously followed a ritual: after waking up, she'd always walk over to our room to visit Elizabeth in bed and play with her. As soon as she came back from my mom's house, she went back to her ritual. Except that now there was no Elizabeth in bed. Worse yet, there was no Elizabeth anywhere—period. At least, not on this plane of existence.

Iz looked at me puzzled.

Now what? How the hell do I handle this? How do I tell a nineteen-month-old baby that she'll never see her mother again? My own thoughts about death are far from clear. How do I explain it to someone else—someone who learned how to speak a few words not so long ago?

And even if somehow she can grasp the meaning of what I need to say to her, how will she handle the emotions that come with it? The overwhelming majority of the adults around me can't handle them. When I explained the situation at the daycare where she spends six hours a week, the teacher broke down crying.

My friend Julio was as tough as tough could get. He had grown up among gangsters in South Central LA, where it was an uneventful month if no one was shot dead on his block. The man was simply inoculated against tears—pretty much nothing fazed him. When I told him what had happened to Elizabeth, he cried like a baby. He hadn't shed a tear in over a decade until then. So, how did I think Iz would react?

The more I thought about it, the less I knew what to say, so after a while I decided to cut the bullshit and say it exactly as it was. I held her in my arms, looked in her eyes and said, "Mama loves you, but she died. We'll never see her again. So, you can stop looking for her because she is not coming back."

I am not sure how I had expected her to respond, but she did react as one may imagine a nineteen-month-old to react when being fed a heavy, highly complicated concept. She appeared distracted. I wasn't sure if she even listened or if she understood anything I had said. Hell . . . even I couldn't fully grasp the meaning of what I told her.

But starting the following morning, she stopped looking. Somehow, she decided to abruptly quit the ritual that had been part of her daily routine for months. Maybe she had understood after all.

Ninety-nine percent of the time, she dealt with the situation in a way in which I could not possibly hope for anything better. But just when I'd think that maybe she was simply not aware of what had happened, she made it clear that that was not the case. One day, as we were walking around the block, we saw an Asian woman getting into a car thirty yards away. Her hair looked very much like Elizabeth's. Iz took off running and tried to dive in the street in an effort to stop her—howling as she saw the car drive off.

And on a different day, in one of the toughest moments of my entire life, I watched her find Elizabeth's driver's license and spend the rest of the morning holding it, kissing it, and rubbing it on her head because that was the closest thing she had to cuddling with her mom.

CHAPTER 35

A Coldhearted Son of a Bitch

"Don't you think it would be better for Isabella to be around someone who looks like her mom? Plus, you haven't had a minute to yourself in the last six months. You need time to unwind and grieve. Let me take her up north with me for a couple of weeks."

A part of me badly wanted to say yes to Belle's proposal. It was probably the same part that craved sleep the way a man who has ventured too deep into the desert craves water. It was the part that didn't care about anything and anyone in that moment, but just wanted to focus on my own needs. But that part got badly outvoted by the rest of me. Bullets have taken longer to explode out of guns than it took me to think about it and say no. Isabella was already going through the shock of having a parent disappear out of her life. As well-intentioned as the idea to take her to Northern California to stay with Elizabeth's sisters may have been, removing her for two weeks from the only parental figure left (yours truly) didn't seem like a good plan.

It's not like I was above asking for help. Quite a few people, for example, were helping out with much-needed money at a time when my financial situation was unraveling quickly. Friends of mine and friends of Elizabeth were generous beyond words. Even people I would never have expected to help volunteered to lend a hand. One day, a letter showed up from Tom Robbins, my all-time favorite novelist, and author of masterpieces such as *Still Life with Woodpecker* and *Jitterbug Perfume*. I had met Tom about a decade earlier, and had stayed in touch since then, but we weren't exactly hanging out on a daily basis. And yet, proving that in addition to being the greatest bard in American literature he was also a sweet gentleman, Tom had dropped in the mail a check for Isabella. My already manic devotion for the man (and for his glorious lady, Alexa) reached new heights.

So, moral of the story: I was all for receiving help. I was just against any kind of help that took me away from Iz.

It would have been legitimate to expect that the second Elizabeth died, I would have finally crumbled, and all those emotions I had kept at bay for months would have exploded. And they probably would have if it weren't for the fact that now I had another mission that required me to be "on" 24/7. Isabella's well-being now rested entirely on my shoulders. Here was a nineteen-month-old baby who had just lost her mom; a tiny human being who depended on me for everything. Taking care of her meant not simply taking care of all her practical needs—from sleeping to food, from diaper-changing to watching her every second of the day to keep her from rolling down a flight of stairs or sticking her fingers in an electric socket or partaking in one of the million activities through which babies regularly attempt infant suicide. Taking care of her also meant making sure she received her daily dose of laughter and positivity. My own emotions and petty dramas would have to wait. My baby couldn't care less that I may be justified in feeling less than enthusiastic about life given recent events. She needed me to be happy and help her find happiness—whether I was in the mood for it or not. Having to be there for her forced me to quit feeling sorry for myself—simply because it would take up the time and energy I needed to make sure she was ok.

It was obvious that a good chunk of the people I interacted with were quite puzzled. They expected me to fall into a deep depression, appear emotionally crushed, crawl into a hole, and cry for a year. Instead, I looked ok—too ok for some people's taste. As some people voiced more or less directly, the way I was reacting was inhuman—perhaps I was just a coldhearted son of a bitch after all. I cracked jokes and laughed a lot. I burned with energy and vitality. I seemed to have lost all inhibitions and was trying to enjoy life in spite of it all.

Is it because I didn't love Elizabeth? Fuck that. I had loved her as much as any man will ever love a woman. But my falling to pieces would not have helped her or honored her memory. I would give myself five minutes a day to cry, feel horrible, and break down right after I put Iz to bed. But once my five minutes were up I'd put myself back together to do what needed to be done. I had a book to write while she slept, and I had to be ready to greet her with a smile the second she woke up. Anything less than that, and I would have been a self-indulgent asshole who put his own psychodramas before the happiness of a baby who craved every bit of positivity she could get.

If from the outside, I may have made it look easy . . . well . . . it wasn't fucking easy. I acted the way I did because what was the alternative? I really didn't have the time and energy to feel sorry for myself at a time when I needed to reinvent my career (which was collapsing), figure out how to save our house (on its way to a foreclosure), and take care of Iz. As later events would make abundantly clear, mine was probably not the ideal way to handle things, but I couldn't see any better options.

My mom lived too far away to be able to help on a daily basis. I was already thankful that she could come watch Iz a couple of days a week while I was at work, but I couldn't ask for more than that. And I was too short on money to afford regular babysitting (friends such as Emily and Jamie Ludovise, Lizelle Legaspi, and the entire Em tribe were ultra-sweet in donating their time, but I didn't want to take advantage of their kindness beyond a minimum). So, Iz and I were pretty much joined at the hip. I remember crying the first time I was able to find a friend I trusted enough to leave her with Iz while I had an hour to myself (not exactly for myself—it was for a doctor's visit).

From my vantage point, it looked like complaining was a luxury. People who whine do so because their life doesn't suck that bad. If it did, they wouldn't have the time and energy to whine, for they'd be 100 percent focused on keeping their nose above the shit trying to drown them. As far as I know, no one is ever depressed during a marathon. And I was very much in the middle of a metaphorical marathon. I had no spare energy to indulge in anger or depression.

Almost every day, something happened that threatened to pull me down into the abyss. I would find a photo album with pictures of Isabella and Elizabeth, and a note in Elizabeth's penmanship reminding me that this was so I would never be far away from them. Or I would be playing with Isabella on the floor, and I would find strands of Elizabeth's hair under her bed. Each time something like this would happen, I felt like a part of me was being ripped away. And yet I knew I couldn't open that emotional door because I still had to be fully functional while moving at top speed. Had I opened it . . . I wasn't sure I would have been able to close it again.

Any time those moods were overtaking me, I'd remind myself that going down that path was not going to help Elizabeth. What

I did instead was try to answer some questions: Since I can't do anything for Elizabeth, what's the next best thing? What would she want me to do? I knew there was one thing she'd want me to do more than anything else: put every ounce of energy into giving Isabella all the love that I could.

ISABELLA INTERLUDE 1

Isabella and Buddhism

Here, in between main chapters, begins a series of stories about the surreal dialogues and episodes that life with my daughter entailed.

Isabella at two years old.

For a few weeks, the first word Isabella would say after waking up was "Buddha." She had turned some wooden Buddha statue into her friend, so every morning she'd go to pet him while saying "nice, nice" and she'd hug him. Her morning routine would continue with breakfast and dancing to Bob Marley tunes.

Her friendship with the wooden Buddha didn't prevent her from yelling at him, though. About half an hour after I had finished gently scolding her for being not particularly pleasant with some visitor who had stopped by, I noticed that Iz had grabbed her Buddha and was reading him the riot act. She lectured him in a stern voice, "You have to be nicer to people, Buddha! You have to be much nicer."

She later proceeded to drop him by mistake, effectively decapitating him. This was the second Buddha-decapitation of her career. She cried like crazy over the headless Buddha until I glued him back together. At that point she hugged him and wouldn't leave him out of sight.

Her curious Buddhist interactions continued during a trip to Starbucks. I didn't even drink coffee, so our daily excursions there were purely done because she enjoyed socializing with the patrons. On this particular day, we ran into a Tibetan monk—probably from the same temple of the monks who came to chant for Elizabeth. Iz walked up to him and immediately improvised a two-year-old version of a long monologue about how she had just washed her toy animals in the bath, how the police were chasing her (I'm not sure why but being chased by the police was one of her recurrent fantasy scenarios), and how she was there to get cookies. The Tibetan monk spoke about three words of English (one of which was "Buddha," another was "coffee" . . . not so sure about the third one) and had no idea what the hell this tiny talkative creature was saying, but he gave her big smiles and a high five. Satisfied with this interaction, Iz walked away to get her cookies. The Tibetan monk, after hearing Iz's "if you play with animals, then wash them," promptly achieved enlightenment.

CHAPTER 36

Writing a Funny, Lighthearted Book While Dangling over the Abyss

Perhaps the Universe thought I didn't have enough on my plate since, in the midst of everything else going on, I was supposed to write a book. Shortly after Elizabeth's health problems had begun, I had signed a contract to write a playful, tongue-in-cheek book about religion on a fairly tight deadline. Obviously, I hadn't been able to even look at it over the last few months, and now the deadline was fast approaching. My days were already filled to the point that I barely had time to sleep, and I only had a few weeks to get it done.

Have fun, Daniele. Maybe if you push hard enough you can squeeze a fifty-hour day into twenty-four hours.

Writing *50 Things You're Not Supposed to Know: Religion* began as a chore but ended up being one of the best things I could do for myself. A few months back, I had just finished writing a giant book entitled *Create Your Own Religion*, that had taken me several years to complete, and I really wanted to see it finally printed. So, when the publisher Disinformation told me they might buy *Create Your Own Religion* in the future, but for now wanted me instead to work on a much shorter book for their *50 Things You're Not Supposed to Know* series, I wasn't all that enthusiastic. I mean . . . hell . . . I gave them a book that had been written with my sweat and blood over the last five years, and they replied by saying, "That's sweet, but can't you instead write for us a little funny book that can be read while on the toilet?"

Their mentioning the magic word "advance" (as in, "we'll send you an advance check in the mail") did wonders to raise my level of enthusiasm, but I still felt a bit like a literary whore since this wasn't *my* book. It looked fun enough, though. Coming up with fifty stories/characters/anecdotes about religion that are little known, bizarre, possibly offensive, and preferably hilarious, definitely wasn't a bad deal. The only issue was the tight deadline, but since my life had not gone to hell yet, I thought I could get it done and gave my word that I would. It's safe to say that I had not anticipated what the universe had in store for me, but here we were.

The guys at Disinformation were very cool to me and said they would postpone the project, but by this point I badly needed the money, and, if at all humanly possible, I never, ever go back on my word. So, I just began to work. Since my free time was nonexistent, I would think about the next sentence while feeding milk to my daughter, while driving, grocery shopping . . . There are entire paragraphs that I dreamed and wrote down word-for-word as soon as I woke up. The second I put her to bed, I'd start writing until I passed out, and start over the following day. Even though this may sound like a punishment, it was the best thing I could do under the circumstances. Sitting around whining and contemplating how much life can suck wouldn't have helped me. By forcing me to focus all my remaining energies on getting the job done, writing the book basically chased away self-pity and all those other forces that drain one's spirit. On top of that, it forced me to be lighthearted and funny about very serious topics—at a time when life was neither lighthearted nor funny: the best therapy for horrendously tough circumstances.

Also, I had always been a pain about writing. I used to spend long hours debating the merits of every single word in the most perverted, perfectionist fashion. Having no time to indulge in this psychosis showed me that the quality of my writing was the same whether I had two or ten hours to get a certain section done. During some seriously fucked-up months in my life, writing *50 Things* allowed me to smile—a lot. After all, I had a chance to write chapters with titles like "Orgies for Jesus," "The Trial of the Zombie Pope," "If You Are Poor, It's Because God Hates Your Guts," "Bible Porn," "Teletubbies Are Gay (And God Hates Them)," "Zen and the Art of Chopping Your Enemies' Heads Off," and "Deadly Alliteration: Moses the Mass Murderer." (About this last one, I seriously hope that the sweet Jewish people who gave my daughter a scholarship to attend their daycare never read this book.) Disinformation (and life's circumstances) removed all inhibitions from my writing. And in dealing with a topic as important and sensitive as religion . . . the result was a lot of fun.

Even more importantly, finishing the book allowed me to write something that was neither funny nor lighthearted, but deeply heartfelt. The book dedication gave me a chance to commit to writing exactly what I was feeling at that time about my lady and my daughter. Here's what I wrote:

To Elizabeth Han:
    In over a decade by your side I have known more happiness and more pain than most mortals could ever dream possible. Our love kicked open the gates of heaven for me. And it thrust me in the deepest

pits of hell. Given the chance, I'd do it all again in a heartbeat. Being with you has meant tasting life to the fullest, since you are/were too damn intense to have it any other way.

Nothing, absolutely nothing in this world is more beautiful than your laughter. From the second I met you to when you died in my arms, you were the beating heart of my universe. My passion for you knows no bounds. In this life or in any another, you are my love.

To Isabella Han-Bolelli:

If it weren't for you, I may not have survived all the heartbreak that a fucked up destiny has decided to throw my way. But you are my hero, baby girl. Your one-year-old smile chases away all the horror, and gives me the strength to move mountains. From the moment you skydived out of your mother's womb into my arms, you have been my reason for living. Looking into your beautiful eyes inspires me to be the best human being I can possibly be. And let's not forget that every one of your burps makes this world a better place.

ISABELLA INTERLUDE 2

Kate Upton

Isabella at two years old.

One morning, upon checking my email I found a message from the director of the Italian edition of *GQ*, asking me if I could take a day to fly to New York to interview a certain Kate Upton. This was right before Upton became a household name. So, not having any idea who she was, I googled her name and . . . damn . . . videos and photos gave me the sense that interviewing her would probably not turn into the worst day of work of my life.

Everything was set up so I could go to New York to meet Ms. Upton. A couple of days before my flight, Isabella got sick. It didn't take more than a few seconds of cussing in multiple languages to know what I had to do. I definitely couldn't leave Iz while she was not feeling well, so goodbye interview—goodbye Kate Upton . . . That fuckin' baby owes me big.

CHAPTER 37

Fist, Please Let Me Introduce You to Wall. Wall, This Is Fist

At times, it seems like the Universe has a personality and does things on purpose. This feeling is probably due to some grossly exaggerated sense of self-importance. The Universe in all likelihood has better things to do than actively intervening in anyone's puny little existence. But this very logical conclusion still doesn't erase the fact that occasionally things happen in a way suggesting the Universe is acting with stubborn determination and clear intention.

In my particular case, the Universe was being a dick. In the span of a few weeks, several things happened indicating the Universe was hard at work, busily trying to fuck up my life.

Elizabeth's death was clearly by far the biggest and most traumatic moment. Anything else paled by comparison, but for good measure the Universe decided to pile things up on top of that anyway. Math can be an unforgiving bitch, and this became painfully obvious with the ugly discovery that there are things you can do with two incomes that you just can't do with one.

Shocking—I know. Specifically, paying the mortgage was never an issue when Elizabeth was able to contribute at least a little money. But now the game had changed and my income alone didn't cut it.

The good news was that at this time, about half the country was having problems with mortgages and the housing crisis was national news. So, most banks were bending over backwards modifying loans in order to avoid having too many unsellable properties on their hands . . . or so we were told.

Apparently, the companies owning my mortgage didn't get this memo. For weeks I spoke with them almost daily, navigating through oceans of bureaucracy in an effort to save our home. I didn't need a huge break, but I still needed one. Thousands of pages of faxed documents later, and after enough jumping through legal hoops that if it ever became an Olympic sport I'd have a shot at the gold, the financial powers that be graced me with a response—two actually, since I received two letters from the bank on the same day. The first, through some highly convoluted legal lingo, told me to screw myself. The explanation was that I was making too much money to qualify for a loan modification. The second also told me to screw myself, but the reason had changed. Apparently, they couldn't help me because I made too little money, so there was no point modifying my mortgage since they didn't believe I'd be able to pay it anyway!

Hell . . . they could at least have flipped a coin and settled on one reason to deny me. Sending two letters with mutually contradictory explanations sounded like a bit of overkill. But regardless, the essence of the message didn't change: Iz and I were still screwed.

Just to prove that bankers do have a heart of gold after all, the head of a smaller bank that owned one of my mortgages reached out to me through some mutual contact. In light of our situation, he'd help us out . . . if I gave him $20,000 under the table. I was livid. Here I was doing crazy things trying to stay on top of my obligations in spite of everything that had happened, and not only did these little shits not move a finger to help, but they tried to profit on my misery? A bribe?!? Really? The head bastard wanted a bribe?

And that's when I decided that they would never see another dime out of me. With no realistic chances of being able to keep the house long term, why even bother paying for a few more months? Had they taken even a tiny step to work with me, I'd have done the impossible to figure out a way to live up to my end of the bargain. But the realization that I was dealing with vampires trying to squeeze blood out of Iz and myself removed any of my moral qualms. I'd fight them every step of the way, employing all tricks in the book to stay in the house for as long as possible.

This would not be an entirely smooth ride: bankers tend to frown on people not paying up, and come after you with a vengeance. At one point, the company that was helping me keep the bank thugs at bay suggested I file for bankruptcy—"file" being the key word. According to the plan, I wouldn't really go through bankruptcy. I would file for it since the simple act of filing would buy me a few more weeks, but I'd withdraw my request before it went through. This actually would have been an excellent plan if it weren't for a tiny detail they forgot to mention. Filing would keep foreclosure at bay, but would also result in my credit cards being cancelled and the money in my bank account being frozen.

So, one day I came home to a letter informing me that between my checking and savings accounts, I now had available a grand cumulative total of $0.00. My father, who had flown in from Italy and was there to help me for a couple of weeks, thought the news would crush me. Instead, I folded up the letter, put it aside, and went on to warm up some milk for Iz and cook some pasta for us. In light of everything I had been through, it didn't seem that important. It was just stupid money. Not only would they probably unfreeze the account in a few weeks, but I could also make more money. It's funny how death puts everything else into perspective. Problems that would seem earth-shattering under normal circumstances are barely noticeable when compared to the ripping of loved ones away from you.

My boxing match with the Universe continued, though. Unhappy that the mortgage-bank-foreclosure-let's-freeze-your-bank-account game had failed to knock me out, the Universe promptly turned to low blows.

For about a decade now, I had been making a living as a part-timer teaching for various universities. Part-time was actually a funny concept, since I taught more classes than full-timers. The classification really has nothing to do with how much you work, but everything to do with job security (or lack of thereof) and pay (lower for part-timers). Joining the rank of full-timers is pretty much what 99 percent of part-timers want since it translates into much better pay and guaranteed work. Students loved me with an enthusiasm that was more than a little humbling for me, and several tenure track professors told me that it was only a matter of time before I'd be hired full-time. The one college where I had the best chances hadn't had an opening in my field for more than ten years, but as soon as they did—I was told—my chances were excellent. The arc of my career for the last decade had been built with this goal in mind.

In the very same weeks when all of this was happening, an opening finally arrived. Maybe, I'd be able to stay on top of my mortgage after all.

Wait . . . what's that sound I hear? I'm afraid it's the Universe laughing in the background.

In their infinite wisdom, the academic bosses decided to turn me down in favor of someone with virtually no teaching experience, but with a PhD from a top ten university. The logic for this was fairly straightforward. I had just been too naïve to see it until now. This choice would allow the college president to go to fundraisers with rich alumni and boast that their last hire was from some top-notch institution—which was supposed to greatly impress them and make them open their wallets for more donations. Never mind whether that was what students actually wanted or not. Never mind whether the person being hired knew anything whatsoever about teaching. These factors had nothing to do with the academic game. And it was my fault for having believed otherwise.

This is why I infinitely appreciate sports: if you are the best in a particular sport, and you keep winning, eventually you'll reap the rewards that go with it. But in academia, quality of teaching had less than nothing to do with who gets hired. I'd have been glad to battle it out with anyone in terms of quality of teaching. And if by any chance they turned out to be better than me, I'd have shaken their hands and gone home knowing they deserved it. The guys from the old guard who had been telling me I'd get hired still operated from the mindset of a time when teaching quality counted for something. Those days were gone. The writing on the wall was that my career likely had no future, and I'd be lucky to continue to get as much part-time work as I had had so far. The door to full-time status, though, was being firmly slammed in my face.

What do you say, Daniele? On the ropes, but not out yet? The Universe suddenly turned into a hungry Mike Tyson deciding to sample one of Evander Holyfield's ears as a snack. Just for the sake of adding gratuitous punishment, It pointed the way to my house to a thief in need of a score. With a thank you to the Universe for the tip, the thief broke into our house when Iz and I went out.

I'm sure there's much worse out there, but being on the receiving end of all this within the space of a short period of time made me feel like I was stuck in a particularly unpleasant Biblical story. You know the charming one where God and the devil get together and wager how much crap they can dump on a poor bastard's life before he decides to smash his head with a rock or something equally fun? Yeah . . . that.

So, my lady was dead. The career I had put together piece-by-piece over ten years came crumbling down in front of my eyes. We were going to lose our home. I was sick with a debilitating mystery illness (more on this later). And now even the damn thief. The Universe was clearly having a blast kicking my ass. Good thing I was used to getting my ass kicked in and out of the ring.

ISABELLA INTERLUDE 3

Iz Is My Hero

Isabella at three years old.

One of the many reasons why Iz is my hero.

Iz: "Mama died."

Me: "I know, baby."

Iz: "I'm sad."

Me: "Me too."

Iz then hugged me tight and added, "I'll put my clothes on and I'll go look for her. I'll say, 'Where are you? Where are you?' and I'll bring her back to you."

This will be a recurring theme in the months and years to come. She once saw a Bruce Lee clip and fell in love. She asked my father a million questions about Lee, and was a bit bummed when she found out that he was dead. But she quickly voiced that she'd save him, would save her mom as well as all the people she loved who had died. She'd bring them all back, and make them happy. With a note of hesitation, she then added, "But I'm little and they are heavy. So, I'll need help carrying them all."

CHAPTER 38

Sipping Champagne among the Ruins

Are you done feeling sorry for yourself, Bolelli? Is the whining over? Jesus, man . . . enough already!

Eventually, my "poor me" moment faded away as I realized I was just wasting energy. It's like events were drilling into me the same lesson over and over: enjoy the ride no matter how rough it is, and if you feel like complaining, use that anger to fight and change things instead. So, it was with a refreshed attitude that I walked into a meeting with Troy Johnson, my friend and department chair at another one of the universities where I worked.

I had met Troy when I was in graduate school at UCLA. At that time he was visiting/teaching there for one semester before returning to his regular appointment at Cal State Long Beach. His was the very first graduate course I took. Within about ten minutes, he had me terrorized. He had picked up teaching after a couple of decades in the Navy. He was in a suit and tie (not exactly my style), and appeared as straight-laced as one could get. Even more troubling was when he told us right off the bat that he expected us to read eighteen books (a minimum of about four hundred pages each) in the following ten weeks.

Who's this crazy son of a bitch? I mused by the end of class as I wondered how I'd survive the workload he was planning to dump on us. I wasn't exactly his biggest fan after that first day. Little did I know that eventually he'd encourage me and guide me like no one else in my efforts to get teaching gigs, would give me a job and continue to keep me employed, thereby making sure that me and my family would be well fed for the following decade. I have no idea what he saw in me or why he decided to help me, but I am eternally grateful that he did.

I knew that the meeting we were about to have was not going to be a particularly happy one. Troy had been putting on a juggling act to keep courses offered despite operating on a progressively shrinking budget. He had been pulling the proverbial rabbit out of the hat more times than I can remember in order to keep giving me work, but the game was up.

As he informed me, the coming semester would be the first since I began teaching that I'd have no work in the American Indian Studies Department. He seemed sadder about it than I was. The department was collapsing before his eyes, and a sense of defeat was hanging in the air. After the ugly news, he immediately jumped into a long strategic monologue explaining all the ideas he had to resurrect the department (and my work) in the near future, but it was abundantly clear that none of them had any chance to succeed. I gently but firmly pointed out this fact, since I don't like false hopes.

He took a deep breath. He knew I was right. He knew it was very probable that none of these efforts would pay off, but was trying to ignore the ugly truth in order to avoid admitting time was up.

"It's ok to acknowledge it's over, Troy. There's no use pretending. I think this is it."

There was no anger or sadness in my voice.

"How long have you been teaching here?" he asked me. "Ten years?"

"Eleven."

"Eleven," he mused. "Well . . . we had a good run, didn't we?"

He was desperately trying to put a smile on his face, but his heart was clearly heavy. If the fact that the department was crashing and burning and that I was out of the main job I had had for the past decade was not quite cheerful enough, there was another reason for the sadness in his voice. Troy had been recently ravaged by his second bout with cancer. Half of his face was falling down. He couldn't control the tears constantly oozing out of one eye. And he was in the middle of waiting for the MRI results telling him if they had gotten it all through surgery or not. Perhaps the "we had a good run" comment referred to more than just the status of the department.

In that moment, a sense of happiness dawned on me. I hadn't completely lost my mind—or, at least, I didn't think so. Yes, the news we were discussing was not exactly happiness-inducing, and yes, we were probably justified if we decided to sit there moping about how everything we had worked at for many years was going down the drain, and how his health was failing. But what was the point? The more I thought about it, the more the smile on my face widened.

I looked straight into his eyes and replied, "We have had a hell of a good run. Thank you so much for everything you have done for me. This past decade has been glorious enough to warrant a celebration. I happen to have some champagne in my office at this moment. Shall I go get it so we can have a toast?"

He looked at me like he couldn't believe his ears, but he began to smile as well. Why not? It was good while it lasted, and all things eventually come to an end, so why not celebrate? There's something powerful about being able to celebrate when you sit on the smoldering ruins of your career. It removes all feelings of self-pity and prevents you from thinking of yourself as a victim. The same goes for many other things. Think of most relationships. When people break up, they often do it with a sense of bitterness and anger. But why? Unless the breakup is a particularly ugly one, why the rancor toward the soon-to-be ex? So, it didn't last. Maybe you changed. Maybe your partner did. There's really no sense in pointing fingers and finding fault. Things would probably be a lot healthier if, rather than assigning blame, people celebrated what they had before moving on.

And so, a few minutes later, champagne glasses were on the table and we were drowning our smiles in bubbles.

ISABELLA INTERLUDE 4

Empathy

Isabella at three years old.

One of Isabella's most evident, innate characteristics is a monstrous level of empathy. I thought I had a highly developed muscle for empathy, but she regularly leaves me in the dust in that department. If anyone is sad within her range of awareness, you can bet she'll be next to them to console them in no time.

On this particular occasion, as I was dropping her off at preschool, she noticed a kid bawling after his mom had left him there.

"He misses his mama," she explained to me, while she walked up to him and caressed his head.

"Your mama will come back," she told him. "Don't worry."

And then, channeling her inner Bob Marley, she added that he shouldn't worry about a thing, that everything would turn out all right.

If you guess which song she was quoting from you'll get . . . well . . . nothing.

CHAPTER 39

Eminem, Medical Marijuana, and Trading Punches with Students . . . The Mystery of Why Academics Don't Like Me

Despite the champagne, in the days to come my mind kept going back to the discovery that quite a few straight-laced scholars among my colleagues didn't like me. Anyone who wasn't a complete dumbass would have known that and understood the reasons, but somehow (perhaps proving my dumbass status) this realization still caught me by surprise. That was naïveté to the tenth power right there.

I am nice to all of them. I know my stuff. Students love me. I open doors for people and say please and thank you. What's not to like?

A mix of ego and stupidity had frozen my brain and prevented me from seeing what should have been plain to see. And so I found myself sitting in my office for hours, moping and wondering why some of my stiffer colleagues disliked me so strongly. That's when it finally clicked.

I stepped out of myself for a second and looked at the situation from the outside—as if I were floating above and watching someone else. There I was in my office with the door open while listening to *Fack* by Eminem (a song that contains rather disturbing lyrics about what can be done with body orifices, gerbils, and a tube). Hanging around my neck were the boxing gloves I had just finished using to exchange punches with a student during an impromptu sparring session in the park while on break between classes. And in my hand was the renewal of my medical marijuana license.

Hmmm . . . let's go over this again . . . Why, oh why, would scholars who smell of staleness and dusty books not like me? I didn't think any of them had ever gone for a gerbil (though you never know), but they definitely had a giant stick up their ass. Everything about me was probably deeply offensive to their sensibility. These were people who were scared of anything they couldn't control, anything that lived and breathed outside of their petty academic playground. Their own sense of inadequacy made them both insecure and hostile to what didn't fall within the limits of their area of expertise—which is to say, pretty much everything. No matter how hard I may have tried to be pleasant and act as if we had something in common, seeing me try to make myself at home among them was like a scene from some old body-snatcher movie. It was only a matter of time (usually very little) before they would notice I wasn't one of them, and they'd start hissing and pointing fingers. It was obvious I didn't belong. Why did I ever think I could fit in?

I thought of Alan Watts, the brilliant writer who, more than any other man in the West, popularized Taoism and Zen Buddhism in the English language. People with no previous exposure usually hit a stumbling block the second they try to read one of the many translations of Taoist and Zen classics. Allusions, paradoxes, the foreignness of some concepts, an unorthodox sense of humor, the many things left unsaid . . . lots of factors contribute to discourage prospective readers and make them give up. And this is where Alan Watts' talent came to the rescue. In his own unique fashion, he managed to explain Taoist and Buddhist ideas without losing their poetry and subtlety along the way. He communicated Taoist and Buddhist insights in ways more easily understandable for Westerners without killing the wonder of it all in the process. He guided adventurous readers through unknown lands, lighting the path along the way. His radio lectures and his many excellent books cracked the door open, introducing Taoist and Buddhist ideas to mainstream Western consciousness.

Not surprisingly, academic philosophers looked down upon him. Ditto for quite a bit of the Zen establishment.

"What we are doing is serious business!" they screamed. "This guy looks like he's having way too much fun! He is frivolous. He is superficial. He is a pop philosopher. He doesn't have a stick up his ass like the rest of us. There's clearly something wrong with him." Most of all they resented that someone like Watts, someone that they considered little more than an amateur in the field, could reach and touch many more people around the world than they could ever dream of. The establishment— it doesn't matter whether it's the scholarly establishment or the spiritual establishment, or any other kind of establishment—is always outraged when outsiders can capture and communicate the essence of their chosen fields better than any insider. Watts had never formally studied for too long under anybody. For the most part, he was self-taught. He never received their rubber-stamped certificate of approval, and for this he could never be forgiven. He had forged his own path, rather than submit to their teachings, and the public loved him for it! The fact that I loved Alan Watts more than any "serious" scholar of Zen and Tao spoke volumes about my relationship with the establishment.

All I had to do was take stock of some of my heroes—people like John Milius, Tom Robbins, Friedrich Nietzsche, Ikkyu Sojun, Caravaggio, Evan Tanner, Robin Hood, Crazy Horse, Bruce Lee, Johnny Cash—to realize that all of them were unorthodox, sometimes in trouble with the law, always at odds with institutions, and allergic to rigid forms of authority. They were very much individuals who carved their own paths. If this was what I was attracted to, how could I expect that the guardians of grey, dogmatic institutions could approve of me? If they liked me, I wouldn't be me.

ISABELLA INTERLUDE 5

Lullaby

Isabella at three years old.

On this particular day, I was watching cartoons with Iz. For once, she was quiet and content, so I decided it was my turn to throw a temper tantrum. Out of the blue, I screamed, "I'm tired! I'm tired! I want a nap! I'm tired!" Spending as much time with her as I did was clearly rubbing off on me.

She looked at me for a few seconds a bit perplexed. Without saying a word, she then took me by the hand, led me to the couch, told me to lay down, and sang me a lullaby. With great tact, she chose not to sing the lullaby I had composed for her ("You are stinky and you smell, but I love you just as well"), but rather something very soothing and sweet in a mix of English and Italian.

CHAPTER 40

Tupac and the Open Letter to Academia

It is safe to say this was not my most diplomatic move to date. But seeing the collapse of my long-term career prospects made me just a tad edgy. And that edginess pushed me to compose what would become a rather infamous letter, which summed up my relationship with the academic establishment. Even though I had some people in mind when I wrote it, on some level it was not directed at anyone in particular. The sad little humans I was interacting with weren't all that important. Had they not been there, they'd probably have been replaced by someone just like them. What I had a problem with were not the specific individuals involved as much as the cauldron of mediocrity and conformism that had spawned them. In any case, without further ado, here's the text of the infamous open letter addressed to the academic world:

> I have felt this way for a long time, but have tried to keep my peace, working under the illusion that if

I behaved like a good boy, I could work to change Academia from within. I always knew I didn't fit in among you. Anybody with eyes can tell we are nothing alike. But I love so much what universities could be that I continued hoping against all evidence that there was a niche for me. Now that the academic powers that be have sent me an unmistakable message telling me in polite terms to fuck off—telling me that the fact that students love me is a mark of dishonor in their eyes, telling me that the fact that I have given my heart and soul to teaching for over a decade doesn't mean shit to them, telling me that I can never get a full-time gig teaching since they much prefer people who look like respectable scholars and who—as all respectable scholars—can't teach or write worth a damn . . . well, maybe now that I have nothing left to lose it's time to say exactly what I think.

I used to say that I have a love-hate relationship with Academia, but being in your company for too long has turned it into a hate-hate relationship. Your crime is unforgivable. Universities could and should be wonderful places where people go to forge their personalities, and acquire the tools to turn knowledge into wisdom. They could and should be places where—as Tom Robbins puts it—we "enlarge the soul and light up the brain." They could and should be such places . . . if it weren't for the fact that they are run by people like you—gloomy ghosts who spend their Saturday nights shining their PhDs and devising new ways to squeeze all joy out of learning.

Every glowing evaluation I receive from my students is another strike against me in the eyes of the bureaucrats controlling the factory that is now academia. The assumption is that if students don't find you dry, boring, and needlessly complicated, you are obviously not doing your job and can't be considered a "proper scholar." What you seem to forget is that "fun" is not the antithesis of serious. It is only the antithesis of boring. No surprises there, though. Your writing and your teaching are reflections of who you are—sorry nerds who were locked up in the library forty years ago and never found their way out. Your cold hearts and soft muscles speak volumes to your students before you even open your mouth. Much heaviness and dust come out of your very souls. Good teaching is meant to inform as well as inspire. But in your hands, academic teaching ends up being a punishment for all involved, and universities turn into obsolete institutions destroying and repressing our students' natural talent rather than educating them. I could go on, but the words of a fine American poet seem the most suited to deliver my parting message to you. In the poetically subtle words of Tupac Shakur: "Fuck you and your motherfuckin' mama."

ISABELLA INTERLUDE 6

Another Day at the Office

Isabella at four years old.

Iz: "Are you going to work?"

Me: "Yes, baby."

She ran to grab a sword and handed it to me with these words of wisdom, "Fight hard. Fight good. And don't let the bad monster hurt you."

I'm not entirely sure what she thinks I do for a living . . . but she's exactly right!

CHAPTER 41

Answering Hopelessness with a Defiant Smile and Raised Middle Finger

My wife left me a gift when she died. She handed over to me a little bit of her fearlessness.

For most of my life, I had been a wimp. I had always been calculating how to minimize risks and avoid danger. I had always strategized and tried to play it safe. Even when I was eighteen or nineteen, I thought and behaved like a damn grandpa—probably much wiser than the average eighteen year old, but also much more restrained. Life's unkind face terrified me. I was scared shitless and wanted do everything in my power to avoid pain, suffering, and death.

And then I learned in the harshest way that no matter how hard I tried to avoid the pain-suffering-death triad, I simply couldn't. All my scheming and strategizing, all my playing it safe, all my fighting to keep the sharp teeth of pain away from me and my loved ones didn't keep me safe. It only kept me scared—under the illusion that I could avoid an unavoidable destiny. In many situations, I had found myself too paralyzed to act as I would have liked, for fear of stirring forces that would unleash hell on me.

Elizabeth gave me a taste of fearlessness by removing all hope. Being by her side when facing a truly hopeless situation removed all the illusions behind which I had been hiding. And hope—I discovered—is what nourished fear in my life. The universe, after all, can intimidate you and scare you with the threat that it'll take something that you value away from you. What happened with Elizabeth demonstrated in unambiguous terms that I could wish, pray, and fight all I wanted, but anything and anybody could be ripped away from me. By now I already knew that everything I valued would eventually be taken, so, what the fuck was left to be afraid of?

Until writing these lines I hadn't fully realized what she had done for me with her dying breath. She freed me to be the person I could be if Fear no longer held power over me. There had always been something tentative and overly cautious in a hidden part of my character—something that held me back. And now it was gone, thanks to Elizabeth.

I'm sure she'd much rather have been here to play with our daughter than having fuckin' rescued me from fear. But we don't get to make that choice. This is not some way to rationalize the horror of her dying. It is definitely not a way to find a silver lining to convince myself that everything happened for a good reason, or that it all worked out the way it was meant to in the end. I am not trying to paint rainbows over her grave and somehow sugarcoat it all. There's still no redeeming quality that can put what happened in a better light. And there's no damned good reason for any of it. But the fact remains that Elizabeth did for me what I could never do for myself.

I felt like a beast that tastes freedom after being confined to a small a cage for too long. I was finally unleashed and could run without this weight on my shoulders—starved for life and adventure. I wanted it all, and wanted it now. There was no longer a point in playing it slow and safe, since I had been abundantly sensitized to the understanding that the future was an illusion, and the only thing I could count on was this very moment.

Whether out of stupidity or deep wisdom, teenagers often act without fear of the consequences. They rarely think of the bad possible outcomes of their actions, and thus are more willing to take risks and go after life with impulsive enthusiasm. I had reached the same state of consciousness through an opposite process. I was all too aware of the bad things that could happen, but I also knew that they would happen regardless of how careful and conservative I was in my choices. The experience of heartbreak had taken me to a place where I decided to enjoy it all no matter how fuckin' painful some parts of life could be. So, no regrets, and no fear of getting hurt because I knew I'd get hurt anyway and there was nothing I could do to avoid it.

When I thought about my life until that point and when I looked around me, I saw fear in all directions. Everywhere I turned I was surrounded by people who were scared—scared of getting hurt, scared of hurting others, scared of rejection, scared to say what they feel, scared of death, scared of being alive. I get hurt every day, but so what? When you let fear dictate your actions, life loses its edge, and that's the only thing that I could not accept.

I think of my hero, 15th-century Zen master Ikkyu Sojun. In a society like medieval Japan, which was extremely regimented, where honor was fetishized, and where the emphasis on reputation and "keeping face" was nearly obsessive, Ikkyu lived his life as the freest of the free. He didn't care for the approval of the Zen establishment, or that of society at large. What anyone thought of him mattered preciously little to him. He didn't care to kiss anybody's ass to gain wealth or power or prestige. In an environment where imperturbability was praised, showing being swayed by strong emotions was seen as vulgar, and sublimating one's passions on the altar of duty was an ideal, Ikkyu embraced living with unashamed intensity. He lived every day as if it was his last.

In a world in which making compromises is the rule, his shocking commitment to live freely, rejecting those artificial rules and social conventions that didn't make sense to him, is liberating. There's something pure and beautiful in someone who doesn't try to project a particular public image, but lives exactly as the person he intends to be. Ikkyu never turned his freedom into an excuse for abusive, self-serving behavior, and in both theory and practice honored the Buddhist precept to avoid hurting others. But he simply refused being chained. Despite experiencing plenty of horror in his time, he was always dedicated to cultivating "joy in the midst of desperation."

Surviving something so devastating had shocked my system, and radically changed me. From that point, I'd live without being restrained by inhibitions that didn't belong to me. Life is too short to live by someone else's rules. I'd continue to follow my own moral code, but as long as I hurt no one, I no longer wanted to be inhibited by social pressures or by my own fears. From that moment on, I saw my reflections in people's eyes, and what I saw was a savage. A sweet savage perhaps, but nonetheless a savage uninterested in behaving how "one is supposed to" or in catering to anyone's expectations.

There's a picture someone took in those days that very much captured my state of mind. With one arm I am holding twenty-one-month-old Isabella with as much tenderness as I am capable of. It's the one place I can give her where she can feel protected and loved. I badly want to shelter her from a world that has not been particularly kind. My other hand, however, has its own agenda, and is offering a middle finger to the camera. I am not flipping off anyone in particular. It's nothing personal. It's simply that the Universe has just tried to crush me, and everything that could go wrong has been going wrong lately. And this is my response. This is my way to answer hopelessness with a defiant smile and raised middle finger. It's my way to refuse feeling like a victim. It's my way of telling the forces trying to destroy me that I am still standing. And that I'm going to fight tooth and nail to have a good time every step of the way until I drop dead.

ISABELLA INTERLUDE 7

Bad Words

Isabella at four years old.

In the car, after I picked her up from preschool.

Iz: "Shit is a bad word."

I debated whether it was worth getting into a discussion about whether there actually are "bad" words or whether they are good and bad depending on how you use them. But since I wasn't 100 percent sure of my own stance on the topic (and since she was four years old), I desisted and simply nodded along.

But Iz wasn't done.

"It's a bad word, so I will not say it in school."

So far, so good.

Then her eyes got wider and happier, "I'll just say it at home."

I couldn't think of a good argument against this flawless logic, so I remained silent. She took it as tacit approval and exploded in a joyful, "Shit, shit, shit, shit, shit!"

After getting it out of her system, she looked at me again and reassuringly added, "I will not say it at school or around other kids."

I think I was supposed to say something, but then again, I'm the one who has a raised middle finger as part of his profile picture on his website, so I opted for a dignified silence.

CHAPTER 42

"He Who Has Learned How to Die Has Learned How Not to Be a Slave"

That bunch of merry, jolly folks who were the ancient Romans firmly believed that nothing screamed "fun family time" like watching two guys trying to disembowel each other with two feet of sharpened steel. For centuries, gladiatorial fights were by far Rome's most popular source of entertainment. Countless movies featuring evil, mentally deranged emperors, heroic unjustly enslaved gladiators, and a bloodthirsty screaming mob have convinced us that ancient Romans were some seriously sick bastards—and that gladiatorial contests were the favorite pastime of a nation of sadists.

To be fair, it's not like this impression is entirely unwarranted. I mean . . . who the hell loves to have a snack in the stands while drooling, watching men forced to kill each other with swords? An obsession with death and a passion for bloodshed are essential requirements for putting gladiatorial fights at the top of the list of your favorite sports.

But if we dig deeper . . . ok, we probably still run into blood-lust. But if we dig much, much, much deeper, we may find out that the fascination for gladiators was spurred by other motives too. And I am not only referring to those aspects that don't fit with the traditional narrative depicting gladiators as poor slaves forced to fight in the arena by evil, rich Romans (for example, the fact that a solid percentage of gladiators were not slaves, but volunteers, or the fact that successful gladiators could retire wealthy, or that some of the hottest women in the empire lusted after them and were their groupies, etc.).

I am talking about philosophical reasons.

I can appreciate that looking for philosophy in the midst of sand, swords, and blood may strike some as delusional. "What philosophy?" some will argue. "This is murder turned into popular entertainment. There's no philosophy here, but only barbarism."

Partially true, and yet . . .

Consider the words of that giant of Roman Stoicism who was Seneca. Far from being a fan of the games, Seneca at times voiced his disgust with the goriness and vulgarity of the arena, but at the same time mentioned gladiators in approving terms. A clue to Seneca's thinking is to be found in this beautiful sentence born from his pen (or whatever it is that ancient Romans used to write): "He who has learned how to die has learned how not to be a slave."

He who has learned how to die has learned how not to be a slave . . . Something really powerful is in these words.

In Seneca's worldview, gladiators were Stoic philosophers more skilled at expressing themselves through sweat and muscles than with words. But this didn't make their example less meaningful. Gladiatorial fights—to Seneca—were a form of Stoicism in action.

The experience of gladiators, after all, was a particularly dramatic version of the human experience at large. Gladiators entered a world where softness and pity were foreign concepts. The vow that all gladiators had to take was to be willing to be burned, bound, beaten, and killed by the sword. Which means that gladiators were in no position to harbor any illusions about the future. Regular human beings can afford to keep the thought of death at bay and continue living their lives as if they were going to last forever. This is clearly not the case, but the lack of an immediate threat is fertilizer for delusions. By virtue of their profession, gladiators inhabited a mental space without any room for thoughts of tomorrow. In order to enter the arena in the best possible frame of mind, despite the possibility of death looming large, they had to let go of any attachments and be completely immersed in the present. For a gladiator, being ready to die at a moment's notice was a way of life.

That's the essence of Bushido right there. As the *Hagakure* indicates: "A samurai who is not prepared to die at any moment will inevitably die an unbecoming death." The gladiator, like a samurai, lived with death as his companion any time he drew breath. Each moment he still walked the earth was a gift from the gods, since any expectation of long-term survival hung by a thread. The constant reminder that each day could be their last put gladiators in a unique frame of mind. What ancient Romans call *gladiatorio animo*—the gladiator's spirit—was the defiant power of someone who had lost any concern for status and profit, who could fight like a man possessed precisely because he was bound to no past or future—someone who had long abandoned hope and fear. The awareness that he'd lose everything and that he couldn't save himself or anyone else injected the gladiator with the power of the damned. Without any thought of self-preservation left, the gladiator was free to fight for the joy of fighting regardless of the outcome. By embracing death in the course of an epic fight, the gladiator redeemed himself from the powerlessness inherent in his condition. Here was the most powerless of men going to meet his fate not like a victim, but with sword in hand and a smile on his face. "No one lives forever," the gladiator would say. "But for now . . . to paraphrase the words of the Red Hot Chili Peppers, let's live in such a way that when death comes even the Reaper cries."

When stripped of all the pomp and spectacle, the essence of the gladiatorial games was found in learning how to laugh in the face of death. It wasn't simply a matter of winning fights. It was about refusing to let hopelessness crush your spirit. In doing battle to the very doorstep of death, the gladiator taught everyone a lesson about how to die and how to live.

Again the *Hagakure* hammers on the same lesson:

> Among other things, the Way of the Samurai requires that he realize that something may occur at any moment to test the depth of his resolution, and day and night he must sort out his thoughts and prepare a line of action. Depending on the circumstances, he may win or lose. But avoiding dishonor is quite a separate consideration from winning or losing . . . The veteran samurai thinks not of victory or defeat but merely fights insanely to the death.

Seen in this light, it becomes easy to understand what Seneca saw in gladiators. The gladiator's ability to stand proud in the presence of hopelessness and annihilation, his drive to remain undefeated even when victory was no longer a possibility, was exactly what Seneca had been writing all along. Gladiators embodied the foundations of Stoicism in their every gesture.

The only difference between life in the arena and life outside of it was time. The latter usually lasted longer, but the outcome was the same. Death awaited all—inside and outside the games. As scholar Carlin Barton wrote, "The universe is an arena where there is no *missio*, no discharge, no hope for mercy or deliverance . . ." So what the gladiator did was face in a particularly dramatic ritualized context the same dark terror that everyone else at some point has to face.

Seneca himself would deal with it courtesy of an invitation to kill himself by the emperor Nero who suspected Seneca of conspiring against him. Unfortunately for Seneca, Nero's "invitation" was not the kind of offer you could refuse. And so Seneca had to open his own veins and soak in a warm bath until he died.

But even the 99 percent of human beings who are not sentenced to fight in the arena or ordered by an evil emperor to slice and dice themselves ultimately have to deal with the same dynamics. Coming to terms with one's mortality is on everyone's agenda, eventually.

And again, here goes Seneca, "He who has learned how to die has learned how not to be a slave." Unless one grapples with the greatest human fear of all—the fear of annihilation—one will always be slave to one's fears. This fear will stalk them throughout their entire lives, holding them back and inhibiting their ability to live fully. The Stoic attitude didn't promise to make the problem go away and remove death from the horizon. What it encouraged instead was the forging of a spirit that can enjoy every second of a mortal life despite the knowledge that each passing second brings us closer to our demise.

Identical to this Stoic paradox is the Tibetan Buddhist practice of the sand mandala. Monks will spend days working with painstaking patience to create an incredibly elaborate painting, progressing one grain of colored sand at a time. After countless hours of labor, when the large painting is completed, people enjoy it for a while . . . before destroying it. The point is not to create a masterpiece that will be kept under glass for ever and ever. The point is to teach a lesson about beauty and the impermanence of life. The monks learn to keep working at it and enjoy the process, despite knowing full well that they will not get to keep it, and that it will last but minutes after it is done. The mandala is not different from life itself. Its amazing beauty is certainly fleeting, but this is no reason not to enjoy it while it lasts. But an excess of attachment will only bring you misery. So, enjoying things for the moment is the Stoic-gladiatorial-Buddhist solution. This, clearly, is almost inhuman and impossible to achieve. The natural human response, after all, is to become increasingly more attached the more we love something. How is it possible to love with full intensity but with no attachment?

I don't know that. I'm not there, probably never will be, and am not even sure I want to be. But loving every damn instant on the planet without the excess of attachment that inevitably brings fear of loss and heartbreak along with it . . . that's an art that everyone could use.

ISABELLA INTERLUDE 8

The Next Jimi Hendrix

Isabella at four years old.

Isabella's musical taste has always been eclectic and a tad unusual for her age. In addition to liking all the Disney soundtracks and the more age-appropriate tunes, by the time she turned two she had become a Bob Marley devotee. I'd regularly catch her humming *Buffalo Soldier* to herself and singing about having been stolen from Africa.

On one particular occasion, after enjoying Disney's *Sleeping Beauty* countless times, Iz told me she didn't like it anymore.

"Why?" I dared to ask.

Iz: "Because there are no Bob Marley songs."

According to her, the movie would have been much better if the prince had woken up Sleeping Beauty by singing *Get Up, Stand Up* . . .

Giving Bob Marley a run for his money in Isabella's heart was good old Jimi Hendrix. Ever since she saw some footage of Hendrix at Monterey playing with his teeth and setting his guitar on fire, Isabella had been captivated. For weeks in a row, a recording of Jimi's *Little Wing* became her lullaby, and *Wild Thing* quickly turned into one of her favorite songs ever.

As a result of her passion for Hendrix, and her desire to know all about him, I had to discuss what a drug overdose was (and had to follow up with a detailed comparing and contrasting session regarding the death of Bruce Lee and the death of Jimi Hendrix). This was not a conversation I was planning to have with a four-year-old, but by now I had realized all preconceptions regarding what a conversation with a kid was supposed to be like had to be tossed out of the window, for Iz was not exactly a typical kid.

One day, while watching cartoons, Iz paused a rerun of Bugs Bunny (who, incidentally, is one of my role models), turned to me, and asked, "How can I take Jimi Hendrix's place? I mean . . . he's dead and someone should play like him . . ."

Time for a trip to a guitar store, then.

Isabella's preference for highly intense music was hard to ignore. Actually . . . that's not entirely true. She clearly adored some mellow reggae, and she could listen enraptured to the sweetest, most romantic songs. She'd love even some classical music (once I saw her tearing up listening to Beethoven). But she also clearly dug loud, explosive, in-your-face tunes. *I Fought the Law* by the Clash was one of the most requested songs any time we were in the car. And by the time she was five, one day she walked into kindergarten proudly singing the lyrics to Joan Jett's *Bad Reputation* about not giving a damn about her reputation, and doing only what she wanted. Good luck to her teacher!

One of the (minor) problems with Isabella's very adult taste in music was her seemingly uncanny ability to pick up the most inappropriate lines in any song she heard—even if she listened to them just once and in passing—and repeat them precisely at the worst possible times (or best, if you are going for comedic effect and don't mind lawsuits). At three years old, she walked up to her teacher and sang "You PMS like a bitch, I would know." (Thanks Katy Perry!) At four, she decided it was a good idea to enter her school while singing "Weed is life. Weed is reality." (Thanks a lot Snoop . . .) In light of this, I promptly struck Eminem and Tupac from my playlist whenever she was around.

CHAPTER 43

Truly Badass Is Having the Strength to Be Kind When Life Is Not

I have fought for long and was a fighter so that I might one day have my hands free to bless.
—Friedrich Nietzsche

One of the ultimate things a human can learn is kindness for their fellow humans.
—Evan Tanner

I really don't know if there's a point to pain and suffering. I am not inclined to think that there is some deep lesson that some higher intelligence is trying to teach us by fucking up our lives and making us miserable. It's entirely possible that there is no inherent meaning in any of this. However, this doesn't mean that it's impossible to create something great *out of* suffering— not thanks to it, but in spite of it.

Dealing with suffering is very much like being tossed off the boat when you don't know how to swim. Chances are excellent that you'll drown, but if not, then you'll probably get out knowing how to swim. The same is true in martial arts and in life.

Getting your ass kicked in the ring and on the mat either breaks you or makes you tougher. Having your heart broken over and over again by life does the same thing on an emotional level. Most people will be stunted by these experiences. Becoming a warrior means using these same experiences that destroy normal people to forge you into a kinder, stronger person.

Many people honestly try to be decent human beings. The reason why they often fail so horribly has nothing to do with lack of good intentions. They are just weak. Frustration, bad luck, fatigue, sickness, and a million other forces chip away at our spirit on a daily basis. Subjected to this kind of pressure, most people break. They turn cynical, mean, defensive, and self-ish. Their good intentions meet a sorry end. If kindness is only supported by good intentions, it will be easily worn away by the inexorable grind of daily life. And before you know it, you turn into another bitter asshole who once meant well.

Everyone can potentially end up this way since everyone has a breaking point. We would have to be severely delusional to believe we are completely immune to these forces. But if you are familiar with a brand of toughness and willpower that have been forged through battle, you will not automatically shut down under pressure, and you may manage to push your breaking point further than most people. So, in this sense, what would otherwise be meaningless suffering can be transformed into weight training for your spirit. If by any chance you manage to find your way out of hell, then you almost owe it to life to apply this newly found strength not only for your benefit, but for everyone else's.

Clearly, the relationship between toughness and kindness is not an automatic one. Plenty of really tough people are any-thing but kind. Some individuals who are truly fearless use this ability purely and only for gaining more power, without the slightest thought for anyone else. Their toughness leaves no room for love, compassion, or empathy. But in my worldview, it is precisely because you know all too well what heartbreaking sorrow feels like, and you are able to feel everyone's pain as if it were your own, that you don't want anyone else to experience it. I am not sure why I feel this way. Pure rationality doesn't require the union of toughness and kindness, since it doesn't necessarily lead to any practical advantages. It just feels right.

I am not saying we have to turn into Mother Teresa's clones and help everyone all the time. Kindness to me shouldn't be an automated reflex, or a conditioned response. I very much cherish having the option of knocking out less than pleasant human beings who spread pain to others without caring one bit. But I like choosing kindness whenever possible.

Regardless of whether you believe in God or not, regardless of whether you believe in an afterlife or not, regardless of which particular political philosophy you subscribe to, regardless of skin color, gender, or religious preferences, kindness matters. It improves our collective quality of life. In the words of the great Evan Tanner, "One of the ultimate things a human can learn is kindness for their fellow humans."

One doesn't have to be fearless to be kind. But if you have learned to walk through hell unfazed, you'll have more power to turn good intentions into meaningful behavior, since most of your energy will not be jailed by the demons of your insecurities and weaknesses. In Lakota culture, the virtues of bravery and fortitude are the foundations for wisdom and generosity. Defeating fear allows you to put kindness on steroids. You'll simply have greater strength to bring happiness to those around you. This is what being truly badass is all about in my book—truly badass is having the strength to be kind when life is not.

I see so much hurt in the faces of good people, so much heartbreak . . . In their eyes I recognize my own hurt. And what I want most of all is to have the strength to take it all away. I know all too well that this is simply impossible, but I still find no greater meaning for taming fear than to develop the tools to take some of the pain away from other living beings.

ISABELLA INTERLUDE 9

Clear Plans for the Future

Isabella at four years old.

On this particular day, when I picked her up from pre-school, Isabella was full of news.

She informed me that a four-year-old boy from her class was now her boyfriend. And she told me that she finally found what career path she would want to pursue when she had grown up. After reviewing all the possible jobs they had discussed at her preschool, she decided she liked none of them. It turned out that a career as a ninja was her true calling. Later in that same week, when she began training for her true vocation, someone asked her, "Are you playing at being a ninja?"

She glared back at them. "I am not playing at being a ninja. I am becoming a ninja."

CHAPTER 44

Commencement Speech, Bolelli Style

Most motivational speeches tell you that if you try hard enough, if you stay true to your dreams, if you fight the good fight, if you are passionate enough, if you have enough willpower to withstand rejections and difficulties, eventually things will work out for the best and all your hard work will finally pay off. This is what the entire self-help industry is based on. It's a sweet message. It appeals to our sense of fairness and justice. And it also happens to be complete bullshit.

Or rather, it can be true only if all of the above goes hand in hand with an insane amount of luck. Without luck, doors will remain closed no matter how much you "think positively" about them opening. The notion that good outcomes await you if only you put in enough effort and desire—the notion that the good guys will always triumph in the end after overcoming seemingly impossible odds—belong on the same shelf with delusional maxims such as "everything happens for a reason."

You are in the wrong universe for that. It's simply not the way things work here.

Most people like to be told otherwise because they can't deal with Life when it shows its ugly face. They have to dress it up, domesticate it, and turn it into a Disney movie—lying to oneself as a coping mechanism. The realization that life can be neither merciful nor fair depresses to the core most of those who are forced to stare at it.

I don't find it one bit depressing. I mean . . . I'd prefer it if things were different, but I'd also prefer it if I was made King of Hawaii. I can live with the fact that the universe doesn't cater to my preferences.

Life is tough. Ok, so what? It's not like there's any alternative, so I won't let life's toughness spoil my good mood (ok, perhaps I won't let it spoil it *most of the time*). I'll do the things I want because they feed who I want to be—regardless of the outcome. I'll follow my visions because not following them for fear that they may not come true equals accepting defeat without even putting up a good fight. Victory or defeat are largely out of my control, but putting up a good fight . . . putting up the kind of fight that makes the earth shake and the gods blush . . . this I can do.

I may fail? Big fuckin' deal. If that is the way the game is going play out, I'll make sure to fail giving every last inch of myself. I'll fail in such a way as to give epic poets enough material for the rest of their careers. I don't make certain choices just because I was told that if I'm a good boy, Santa will reward me. I'll make them because living somebody else's life out of fear of failing brings me no joy.

If the universe ends up being kind to your efforts, good for you. But the key question in my mind is: are you willing to make the exact same choices even if—as it's entirely possible—no reward is there for you at the end?

Now you know why I will never be invited to deliver a commencement speech.

ISABELLA INTERLUDE 10

Mulan and Being Like Other Girls

Isabella at four years old.

Iz was singing a song from *Mulan II* entitled *I Wanna Be Like Other Girls*. She was all happy for a while, then abruptly stopped and looked puzzled.

"What?" I asked.

Iz: "I like the song but I don't like the meaning."

Me: "Why?"

Iz: "I don't really wanna be like other girls. I wanna be like me."

CHAPTER 45

No Thoughts, No Swimming Trunks

It's 3 AM and the lights by the Mare Piccolo beach are shining just for me.

Perhaps this is not entirely true: a few seagulls and a stray dog are up and about, but there isn't a single human who is awake in this part of town. It's the middle of summer in Sestri Levante, Italy. In an experience that is rather foreign to me since Iz was born, I don't have to sleep lightly so I can hear her call, and I don't have to worry about passing out early so I can be there for her at some ungodly time in the morning. It's the first time she has come with me to Italy, and she's now sleeping in the next room close to her grandfather. I am on the balcony of my room, enjoying the silence, the smell of the sea, and a moonlit view of the Mare Piccolo beach.

The presence of the sea so close to me is exhilarating. Over two thousand years ago, Roman ships sailed from these shores. I've grown up spending my summers swimming in the Mediterranean, and yet it has been almost twenty years since I dipped my feet in its waters. Airfare is too damn expensive to travel in summer, so my Italian trips have been limited to winter visits.

But this is the first post-Elizabeth summer, and both Iz and I can use some time to hang out with her grandfather.

Over the past several years, I have been having many dreams of swimming in the Mediterranean. I'd always wake up from them with a lingering sense of happiness mixed with longing. And now I'm here. The waves are crashing just a few hundred feet from my balcony. The smell of the sea fills my nostrils. I have missed this so much.

My logical mind reminds me that it's 3 AM and the water is probably chilly. A couple of hours ago, I saw some teenagers jumping in and cussing quite creatively about the freakishly cold temperature. I should really join the ranks of those who have already closed their eyes and are deeply asleep. Tomorrow I can buy myself some swimming trunks and finally dive among the waves. But tomorrow is still far, and I really want to feel the waves on my skin right now.

I used to always listen to my logical mind, but I am not the same man I was just a few months ago. I think less and act more. I am done being so cerebral and careful. So, screw my logical mind and screw my lack of swimming trunks . . .

A minute later my clothes are on the sand and I am naked and freezing in the water. I feel 100 percent alive—100 percent present to the magic all around me. The only sounds are the waves and my own breathing. The reflection of the moon plays with the reflection coming from all the lights of the homes overlooking the beach. And there isn't a single human to appreciate this but me.

Part of the excitement is not just the result of a frozen, adrenaline-filled, middle-of-the-night swim. Much of it comes from not recognizing myself anymore—from having no idea how this new person who is me is going to react to things. I am amused observing this new me. What I have gathered so far is that he is a crazy motherfucker who dives headfirst wherever Life is—very much unlike the "me" I was until recently.

Just a few days prior to the night swim, I noticed the same tendency during the presentation of a book of mine just published in Italy. During the Q&A, many people asked some highly complex questions about philosophy and religion. My answers would come out the second the question ended—complete spontaneity with little interference from my rational mind. The same thing happened tonight. I think of diving in the water, and the next moment . . . Plop! I'm in. No pause between impulse and action.

The same thing happens a few days later. Our flight back to the US turns into a minor nightmare when we arrive in Atlanta to catch a connecting flight to LA, and Delta Airlines can't find any record of the second leg of our trip. As they "work to resolve the situation," our flight departs without us. More digging by Delta employees is equally fruitless, and they make us lose the next flight too. There's only one flight left before the end of the night. If we don't get on that one, we'll have to spend the night in the airport with the hope that they'll be able to fix it in the morning. No one seems the least bit interested in helping us. I look at Isabella who's completely wiped out from the many hours of flying and waiting since we left Italy, and I take in all of her frustration. She's a two-year-old who doesn't know what's going on and just wants to go home.

A quick assessment of the situation tells me that my ability to give a fuck about keeping a dignified public persona has left town about the same time my wife's heartbeat left the planet. Screw it . . . my baby is going to sleep in her bed tonight one way or another.

I hand Iz into the arms of my mom's husband who is traveling with us, and ask him to make sure she's distracted and playing so she won't be alarmed by what I'm about to do. Once that's set, I flop to the floor and fake a heart attack. I twitch on the ground so much that it's not entirely clear if I'm going for a heart attack or an epileptic seizure, but either way it catches the attention of a Delta manager. We are in the US after all. Suing people is a national sport. Dogs may have the best noses for smelling food, but corporate managers are second to none when it comes to smelling lawsuits. Within five minutes, he miraculously finds the record of our Atlanta to LA flight and puts us on the plane.

As I sit on our flight with Iz finally asleep in my arms, one thing becomes obvious: I don't know what the life of the new "me" will entail, but it is safe to say that it will not be boring.

ISABELLA INTERLUDE 11

Dog Costume

Isabella at four years old.

Iz: "I want a dog costume, my size."

Me: "Why do you want that?"

Iz: "Because then I can piss in the street and no one will say anything."

Impeccable logic.

CHAPTER 46

Don't Throw Away the Hero in Your Soul

"It doesn't matter what mood you are in. It doesn't matter if you had a bad day. It doesn't matter how exhausted or mad you are. And it doesn't matter what she has done. You are the parent and she's a little kid. You just can't do shit like this."

After everything I had been through, I was a ticking bomb. Part of me was itching for the moment when someone would cross a line, and I could feel justified in removing their head from the rest of their body. I was just waiting for a good excuse that would allow me to explode and let out all the anger, hurt, and pain that had been bottled up inside. Anyone criticizing me about how I was raising Isabella clearly must have had a death wish.

And yet I took it meekly, without opposing resistance or saying a word. He was right and I was an asshole. There was really nothing for me to say.

My silent admission of guilt didn't push him to ease up on me. He wanted to make sure the message came through loud and clear. Julio had been my friend for about a decade. He had been my student and had looked up to me as some sort of father figure in his life, but this didn't give him any second thoughts about letting me have it.

I had stopped by to pick him up at his place. By the time we had pulled over at his house, Iz was throwing a fit. She clearly didn't feel like being in the car and was voicing her displeasure with loud, rightful indignation. Her screaming managed to touch a raw nerve in me. It had thrown me over the edge, so I responded by yelling at her in the deepest, angriest voice I could muster. Iz's screaming stopped dead in its tracks as she froze up, freaked out by my reaction. Hence my feeling horrendously guilty. And hence Julio reading me the riot act about not traumatizing kids. It took balls of iron for him to do it. Only a real friend would kick your ass so bluntly about something so sensitive.

In the months since Elizabeth's death, my priority number one (and probably two, three, and four as well) had been to ensure Iz's happiness. Everything else—including my own emotions—was just petty bullshit. Despite my best intentions, on a regular basis I'd run into moments when all my frustration, tiredness, and pent-up anger would push me past the breaking point and I would snap. And one thing you can always count on is babies' ability to push your buttons. They don't have to be bad babies for that to happen. Even the best will do that. It's part of their job description.

Any time Iz pushed all the right buttons and I blew up, I'd always end up seeing the same thing: I would see pure panic in her eyes because she had seen a monster. And the monster was me. There was simply no excuse for me exposing her to that. I probably had plenty of reasons to be overwhelmed, and the worst I ever did was raise my voice, but still . . .

It's not like I believe you should never raise your voice with a kid. There's a time and place when that may be the right thing to do. But the way I did it was charged with far too many ugly emotions. Afterwards, I always felt like the worst human in the world.

Once, as I was putting her to bed around the time she was a little past two years old, she hugged me, looked me in the eyes, and said, "You are such a good dada." Considering there were many moments when I felt like anything but a good father, her words moved me to the core. She made me take a real, hard, good look at myself, and strengthened my determination to fight my demons with every last ounce of energy I had. She deserved nothing less.

My case may have been slightly different from others, but in a way everyone is fighting the same battle every single day. It's the battle that the best part of us fights against our selfishness, weakness, and meanness. It's the battle to try to live as the best human you are capable of being. Whenever we lose that battle (and everyone at some point loses), it's easy to get cynical and want to bury our heads in the sand, so as not to have to constantly struggle anymore. Being the hero of your own life is damn hard work. And giving up can look appealing whenever we slip and fall short of our ideals. But the people who will pay the price for our failure are those closest to us.

Good old Nietzsche wrote,

> I have known noble ones who lost their highest hope. And since then they looked down on all high hopes ... Once they thought of becoming heroes; but to them now the hero is a source of shame and fear. By my love and hope I beg you: don't throw away the hero in your soul! Maintain holy your highest hope!

Hell ... those are powerful words. "Don't throw away the hero in your soul! Maintain holy your highest hope ..." I think about those words nearly every day since the first time I read them when I was sixteen years old.

It is easy to forget our highest ideals when sinking in the quicksand of dark emotions, fatigue, and plain bad luck. Given a choice, everyone would want to be an amazing human being. What stands in between the ideal and the real is the monstrous amount of hard work required. Everyone has hero moments— moments of "flow" when we can do no wrong, and we truly embody our highest hopes. But it's one thing to have them when everything is going well, and it's relatively easy to put your best face forward. And it's a whole other thing to be able to bring this forth in the worst circumstances. Can you still live up to your ideals when you have had minimal sleep for weeks? Can you do that when rage and heartbreak threaten your sanity? Can you do that when all around you is chaotic and terrifying? No one—not even the best human out there—is able to live up to the ideals 24/7. What the best human does, though, is fight for it with everything he has and everything he is. The margin between embodying what Nietzsche calls "the hero in your soul" and manifesting a whiny little shit who makes everyone else suffer because of his or her failings is razor thin.

In light of this, every time Iz looks into my eyes, wordlessly reminding me that she needs me at my best, the battle begins again. So, shove your excuses, and do what needs to be done, motherfucker. Truly, nothing is more important than this.

ISABELLA INTERLUDE 12

A Four-Year-Old Dose of Reality

Isabella at four years old.

A conversation between Isabella and an adult.

Iz to the adult: "Where is your mama?"

Adult: "She is no longer with us."

Since this person's mother wasn't in the room at the beginning of the conversation, Iz was puzzled. "No longer with us" . . . what did that even mean?

So, she asked again: "Where is she?"

Adult: "She passed away."

That's another euphemism that went way over Isabella's head.

Iz: "But where is she?"

Adult: "She's now with God in Heaven."

Iz thought about it for a while and countered: "That's different from my mama. My mama died because she had an illness."

CHAPTER 47

Goddesses of Mercy

How the hell did I end up there? In the midst of grief, my life collapsing all around me, and hardly the time to catch my breath, there I was—in a bed, gently holding in my arms a naked woman I had never met until an hour earlier . . .

How did things get to this place?

I am told that some things are better left unsaid. I am told to consider what others would think of me. This advice is quite well intentioned and comes from people who want what's best for me. But everything I have been through makes it impossible for me to follow it. I am not a damn politician trying to present a respectable front. I am not trying to win a popularity contest. Once upon a time I may have thought in terms of how I wanted others to see me. That was before being slammed in the face by the Universe, and being forced to realize that life is too short to worry about upholding a public image. The days of striving to live up to other people's expectations are over. I'm not in the business of Disneyfying who I am. People lie and clean up their image because they are afraid of who they really are, worried of other people's judgment, and ultimately ashamed of themselves.

I am not. I certainly was in the past. No longer. I crave authenticity. I crave radical honesty. I crave the freedom to embrace all of my experiences—the great moments, the painfully stupid ones, and the many ones in between. I may be an idiot at times, and I may not always make the best choices, but I am done editing my life for fear of how others will perceive me.

Which brings us to the naked lady in my arms.

For months, my entire existence had been made of equal parts of pain, grief, taking care of Isabella's needs almost every minute of the day, and working like a dog to keep us afloat. I did it all without complaints, but I was running on fumes. I had turned into a machine running a never-ending marathon. I couldn't even remember the last time I had done something purely for pleasure. There was simply no room in my life for mindless enjoyment.

Speaking of mindless enjoyment, good old-fashioned sweaty sex was probably the only thing that could put me—at least for a little while—in a mental space where thoughts of sickness and death couldn't enter. Sex has no patience for self-commiserating. It leaves no room for wondering about the future or regretting the past. It's the ultimate dose of happiness in the here and now. By now, it seemed like a distant memory—like the shadow of a happy dream upon waking up. My body no longer knew what it felt like, and yet it was the only thing to make me feel like maybe I was still among the living.

The possibility of getting into a romantic relationship was off the table for multiple reasons. My heart and soul were still tied to Elizabeth in such a way that there wasn't any room for anyone else. But even in a distant future—if things were to ever change and I could end up in a place where I could make room emotionally for someone else—how could that ever work anyway? Isabella would be my first, second, and third priority.

Any woman interested in a relationship with me would have to accept that, and most ladies typically are not enthusiastic about becoming the fourth or fifth priority in their guy's life. Never mind the fact that it really wouldn't be fair to ask that of anybody. So, the reality was that it would be many years before I could have the time and energy to dedicate to someone the way one should in a relationship. I'd never want to mess with anyone's feelings, lead them on, and half-suggest something I could never deliver.

I wasn't into one-night stands either. Too often people say they are ok with casual sex only for things to end up much more complicated anyway. The opportunities were all around me, but I just had no desire to take them. Hurting someone in any way was the last thing I wanted.

And yet, despite the fact that I wanted neither a relationship nor a one-night stand, I badly needed the touch of a woman—a simple moment of joy to remind me that there was still beauty in the midst of all the horror.

A possible solution to my dilemma showed up as I was reading about the life of my idol, 15th-century Zen master Ikkyu Sojun. Throughout his life, in fact, Ikkyu openly and unashamedly patronized brothels. This both horrified me and intrigued me. I was never attracted by the idea of separating sex from emotional connection. And the men seeking prostitutes, in my mind, weren't exactly the types capable of healthy relationships with women. Ikkyu's passion for hookers messed with my mental categories since he radically broke away with the sexism typical of the Zen of his days by teaching female students, included a lady he was madly in love with in his official portrait (something that no Zen master had ever done), and was generally renowned for being far ahead of his time in his attitude toward women. His adventures in the brothels were not some kind of deep dark secret he was trying to hide. He simply saw no contradiction between treating women better than 99 percent of his contemporaries and enjoying sex with prostitutes.

In light of this, I had to wonder . . . was I simply close-minded and ruled by prejudice? Could it be that my beliefs on the subject were the result of indoctrination by a moralistic society? For the first time in my life, I considered finding out.

It appealed to me that I wouldn't be messing with anyone's emotions. I simply hate the weird games people play in order to get sex, or the way in which sex is used as a bargaining chip. Most of all, I hate the idea of people approaching sex with different expectations, and someone walking away emotionally wounded as a result. The sex-for-money equation almost felt more honest: there would be no lies, no illusions, no one getting hurt.

This was probably destined to remain a theoretical exercise, since every last cent I had was going into taking care of bills. Except that just as I was grappling with these thoughts, a friend mailed me some money as a gift. The gift came with a condition attached to it, though: the money was his contribution to my mental health—this was not to be used to pay bills or take care of any other practical worry. It was not to be spent on anything but something that would give me a brief vacation from the brutal intensity of my current life.

In the go-for-it-now-ask-questions-later approach that characterized my decision-making at the time, I started look- ing into it. One thing I knew for sure was that I wanted no part in the exploitative, nasty conditions often attached to the sex-for-money business. No street prostitution, no intermedi- aries taking most of the money from the women, and no one making decisions for them. As my homework would reveal, this wasn't as impossible to find as I had been conditioned to think. In plenty of cases, the sex-for-money business is abusive and degrading. But in just as plenty, it's not. A lady in that business I once chatted with told me she had a successful day job, spoke five languages, and had graduated in Anthropology from UCLA. She screened her clients very carefully and rejected more than she accepted. Sex work for her was a form of fun dating while making bank in the process. Clearly, this was not the norm of the business, but stories like this were less rare than I had imagined. After enough digging around in an underworld that apparently existed everywhere around me without me ever noticing, I ran into something that fit my criteria, and decided to take the plunge.

By the time I parked outside the lady's place, I was scared to death. I felt like throwing up and was tempted to call off the whole thing.

"This is not me," I kept thinking. "This is not me. What the hell am I doing here?"

I had zero ideas what to expect, and the prospect of going through with this terrorized me. The possibility that this was not what I pictured in my most optimistic imagination, but that I'd find myself in the middle of something terrible, froze me in place.

But then again . . . after all I had been through, what was I scared of?

Suppressing all my instincts that were screaming at me to run away, I managed to walk up and knock on the door. An amazingly beautiful woman opened the door, hugged me, and kissed me—not some over the top, porn-type of kissing, but something soft and dare I say . . . sweet? The entire interaction was completely unlike anything I had imagined. There wasn't a hint of sleaziness about any of it.

After all was said and done, we laid in bed together, holding each other. The overall vibe was almost tender. I wasn't so delusional as to think that this didn't revolve around a money exchange. We were both very much aware of that. But this didn't mean we couldn't be ridiculously nice to each other. As we relaxed there in the first moment of true relaxation I had experienced in months, she started asking questions about my life.

"Well . . . if you really want to know, I'll tell you."

I wasn't planning on volunteering this information, but since she brought it up I told her everything that had been going on with me. By the time I was done with my story, she handed me my money back.

"You need it more than I do," she said.

This sparked one of the most surreal conversations I had ever had about money as we began politely arguing—each of us trying to give cash to the other. I am fairly sure this is not what most money disputes in the sex-for-money business are usually about. In an effort to make her point, she told me how much money she earned in a year: it was almost three times my yearly income. This particular moment, this counterintuitive argument about money, was by far the sweetest thing that had happened to me in ages. There was more selfless altruism in this brief interaction than in some "real" relationships. She genuinely wanted to help me, and I wanted the same for her. After enough back and forth, we smiled and settled on a compromise about money, agreeing to meet each other halfway.

A few days later, I ran into a friend who had been quite insistent about the idea that I should see a grief counselor.

"You look so much better than the last time I saw you. You seem relieved. Did you see a therapist?"

I hesitated. I knew she was trying to help. I didn't want to hurt her. And I had the feeling that telling her that rather than having a session with a licensed therapist, I had had one with a sex worker, would probably confuse her and anger her.

I appreciated the word "therapist" in her question since it was vague enough that I didn't have to fully lie.

"Yes," I replied with a big smile, "I saw a therapist. You were right. It helped a lot."

And it actually really did. By helping me find a moment of happiness while in hell, by offering unexpected kindness in what could have been a potentially ugly interaction, it helped me tremendously.

Now that I had sworn off relationships, was this going to be my future? Would I return to the comforts of ladies for hire again and again?

It could have turned out that way. But something that my friend Aubrey Marcus told me stirred me in a different direction. I was explaining to him how I wasn't planning on pursuing any relationships—not just now, when the emotions were still fresh, but even in the foreseeable future. I told him I dreaded the possibility of bringing a woman into my life, of the relationship eventually ending, and of my having to tell my daughter, "Sorry that this other female figure you have grown incredibly attached to has also disappeared out of your life and you'll never see her again." I truly thought that I was doing the right thing to protect her. Aubrey replied with few, poignant words that made me do an instant 180.

"You don't hurt kids just by what you expose them to," he said. "You also hurt them by what you don't expose them to. If you never let your daughter see in front of her the example of a loving relationship, you'll not be doing her a favor."

When a man is right, a man is right.

This didn't mean I was going to rush into anything. Not only was I not ready, but I never again wanted to have to modify who I was for the sake of fitting into a relationship. The only plausible scenario would be one in which I could be 100 percent the person I wanted to be. My standards would remain insanely high. And any woman would have to accept that my daughter was the center of my life. The odds were that I wouldn't find something like this easily, just across the street. But the possibility was back on the table.

ISABELLA INTERLUDE 13

Orlando Furioso

Isabella at four years old.

Most kids like to have their parents tell them stories when they go to sleep. Iz was no exception. Whenever bedtime rolled around, Isabella always wanted to listen to my stories. At some point after turning four, however, she told me, "I still want them, but no more kids stories."

Ever since my father—during one of his visits— decided to put her to bed telling tales from the *Iliad* and the *Odyssey*, Iz decided she wanted "big people stories."

So, for a couple of months afterwards, every night I'd summarize for her a chapter of the greatest Italian epic poem ever written, *Orlando Furioso* by Ludovico Ariosto.

The whole book is over a thousand pages and begins with these lines:

"Of ladies, cavaliers, of love and war,

Of courtesies and of brave deeds I sing."

In those two lines there was everything that I had ever been interested in. Iz apparently was equally intrigued with powerful epic tales.

CHAPTER 48

Tequila Pull-Ups

For about two decades, martial arts practice had been my main ritual. It kept me physically sharp and mentally sane. The mat and the ring were my church. Several times a week I'd worship at the temple of the war gods, and walk away feeling refreshed and renewed (and probably bloody and bruised, but that's a different story). All of this changed with the birth of Isabella and with everything that had happened since then. For the first time in my adult life, months went by without any training whatsoever. Then I'd get a day in before more months of nothing.

So, on the day when a friend agreed to babysit a couple of times a week to let me begin training again, I was in heaven. (Thank you, Liezel!) I mean . . . for far too long my only training regimen had consisted of playing with Iz, using her as a kettlebell and doing tequila pull-ups. The tequila pull-ups—in case you are wondering—were my proud creation: every fifteen pull-ups, I'd take a shot of tequila. After putting Iz to bed, I'd typically spend the night writing and using a pull-up bar installed over a door. By the end of the workout, I was fairly buzzed and slept like a baby. It was definitely fun, but not exactly training like a pro. After being glued to Iz 24/7, and spending my days watching cartoons and playing with dolls, in order to redeem any semblance of masculinity (and some mental sanity), I was in dire need of trading punches with heavily tattooed guys.

My return to martial arts was much more fun in my imagination than in reality. Being used to high technical and stamina standards, I was not thrilled to find out how far I had slid. My reaction time was off, my stamina was what you may expect from a guy whose idea of working out was tequila pull-ups, and my technique was sloppy. I knew I wasn't going to be as good as when I left, but this really sucked. I was beyond horrible. After getting schooled by a relatively low-level fighter, I even managed to get injured when he cranked an armbar much too fast. By the time I walked off the mat, I felt like shit—both physically and mentally. This was supposed to be the key to recovering my mental sanity, and instead it depressed the hell out of me.

Quite a few other parents I interacted with suggested more or less directly that it was time to grow up and forget about fighting. Part of me was feeling so low that it was tempted to agree. I never wanted to feel like I did that day again (if this sentence sounds familiar, yes, I do listen to Red Hot Chili Peppers a lot.) After wallowing in self-pity for a few hours, I lifted an imaginary middle finger toward those advising me to quit training. I knew that as soon as my arm healed, I'd be back. For better or worse, fighting was my favorite way to test my willpower and shape my personality.

When, a few weeks of training later, my stamina and technique were on point again, strange thoughts began floating in my head. There was an excellent chance that my teaching workload in college could get slashed to the point where I'd be flat broke. I already wasn't too far from it. I really didn't know what to do for money.

Then the solution to my problems seemed to arrive on a golden platter. I was offered a well-paid job to teach at a fancy, private high school mostly frequented by the kids of the Hollywood elite. Considering everything else in my professional future seemed to be going to shit, this was a gift from heaven. Problem solved then, right? Not exactly. Accepting it meant I'd leave home before Iz woke up, only to be back two or three hours before she went to sleep. She no longer had a mom, and now her dad was going to disappear for the vast majority of her waking life. As much as it pained me, I didn't have to think twice about saying "thanks, but no thanks" to that offer. Whatever I was going to do for money couldn't take me away from Iz too many hours per day.

Partnering in a grow operation for a medical marijuana dispensary helped out a little bit, but the whole thing was too small scale to make a big difference. I put together and sold an instructional DVD about leglocks (by far, the best part of my martial arts game). Again, it was better than nothing, but not exactly the solution to my economic woes. At this juncture, some insane part of me began thinking back to what people had been telling me for years: "If you put in enough training, you are talented enough to do well in MMA." I had no illusion of being able to compete at a top level and still spend plenty of time with Iz. At the highest level, MMA is like any other job: you have to put in the time. But I had the tools to clean house at the lower levels of pro MMA without having to train away from Iz all day long. I didn't need to climb the ladder all the way. I was too old to have the time to do it anyway. All I needed was to pick up a little extra cash by fighting for the smaller promotions where the talent pool was not particularly deep . . . It seemed like a good idea at the time, so I began to spin the wheels to make it happen.

It didn't take me long to catch the interest of a promoter. When I told him that I was still a little rusty, he assured me that my first opponent would be an easy one. He was supposed to be a mediocre amateur who had recently decided to turn pro. The wonders of YouTube showed me that the guy was actually a very well-accomplished pro who had already fought in several countries. The videos testified to some good kickboxing technique and a solid judo background. He was about my level, except that the footage was a year old, and in the meantime he had probably spent that year training his ass off, while I was . . . well, you know what my year was like.

I couldn't blame the promoter for trying to set me up any more than I'd blame a shark biting me when I'm bleeding next to him. Inspired by the "why not?" attitude that had been spurring me along over the past few months, I was tempted to take the fight anyway. But this was different. Yes, I could pick up a sponsorship and make a little cash, but I couldn't really afford to get seriously injured. Getting injured is always a very real possibility when fighting, but at the very least I should limit the odds by being more prepared than I was at the moment. If I got hurt, who would take care of my daughter? If I couldn't pick her up for a few weeks, or even a few days, because I had busted my hands or my legs, no one else would be there to take care of her.

MMA wasn't going to pan out after all. It had been a stupid, desperate idea. Too bad . . . I had been looking forward to walking up to the cage to *Barbie Girl* by Aqua. The look on the faces of those in the crowd would have made it all worth it.

Mama Dreams

Isabella at four years old.

On this particular morning, Isabella looked extra tired.

Me: "What happened, baby? You didn't sleep good?"

Iz: "No. It was impossible to sleep with all that noise."

Me: "What noise? I didn't hear anything."

Iz: "My spirit and mama's spirit in my heart were kissing so loud during the night that they didn't let me sleep. I kept telling them to be quiet, but they ignored me and kept kissing and kissing."

CHAPTER 49

The Most Glorious Sixty-Two Seconds in the History of Moviemaking

"This is the best pizza I have ever had in Wales," I commented, munching down the last bite.

"You have been in Wales for only two hours," retorted my father.

"True. But the chef doesn't need to know that."

Thus, with my arrival in Wales began a very unlikely journey that would lead to unexpected destinations.

In 2012, *I Am Bruce Lee* broke all audience records for documentaries on Spike TV. Its kickass cast included Bruce's family (his daughter Shannon and wife Linda), his top student Dan Inosanto and his daughter Diana, authors Paul Bowman and Teri Tom, boxing champions Ray "Boom Boom" Mancini and Manny Pacquiao, NBA star Kobe Bryant, MMA greats such as Gina Carano, Jon Jones, Stephan Bonnar, Cung Le, and UFC president Dana White, actors Ed O'Neill and Mickey Rourke, grappling legend Gene LeBell, and . . . yours truly.

The strange tale of how my goofy Italian self ended up in this star-studded production began several months earlier, before all the horror and drama began, right after the above-mentioned pizza-eating session in Wales.

I was on a rather desperate mission to see if I could bypass the gloomy ghosts of American academia, and get my PhD through Cardiff University instead. Not that I thought getting a PhD meant anything. It wasn't going to make me a better writer, a better communicator, or a better teacher. And I certainly wasn't doing it for my ego. The only thing it would do was open up more opportunities to land full-time teaching gigs in college. It was purely a means to an end. I saw myself as an academic ninja hiding in their midst just long enough to steal the piece of paper that I needed to do what I wanted.

Upon my arrival, I found out that Paul Bowman, a professor at Cardiff, had dedicated a chunk of his book about Bruce Lee (*Theorizing Bruce Lee*) to argue against some of what I had written in my first book, *On the Warrior's Path*. Since I was there already and I had some time to kill, it seemed only natural to go pay Mr. Bowman a visit.

The look on Bowman's face when I knocked on his office door and introduced myself suggested that he might have thought I was there to kill more than just time. I'm sure he had watched *The Godfather* enough times to know that crossing seemingly polite Italians was a bad idea.

Has this crazy Italian bastard traveled to Wales just to settle a score? It's highly possible that this was not the question floating in Paul's mind, and that my Godfather-assumptions are entirely made up, but since I have no way of knowing and my version is more fun than possible alternatives, I'll stick with it. I felt like I was in that scene from *The Godfather Part II* involving Don Corleone and a landlord . . . the less I said and the more polite

I was, the more Paul felt the need to be extra nice to me. He probably knew that a shotgun was hiding behind my smile. Long story short, by the time I left his office we were on excellent terms.

Fast-forward many months later, and I received a call while I was feeding Iz, and at the same time trying to write the next sentence for *50 Things*.

"We are shooting a documentary about Bruce Lee and we need someone to discuss his philosophy. Paul Bowman highly recommended you and your book *On the Warrior's Path*. Are you free to shoot tomorrow? We could schedule you between Kobe Bryant and Gina Carano."

As much as I would have preferred shooting *with* Gina Carano (preferably while frolicking in a pool of liquid chocolate), there were worse things in the world than accepting this invitation.

After some creative scrambling to secure a babysitter for Iz, the following morning we shot a two-hour interview that would hopefully give them a few seconds of usable footage for the documentary. Shortly after walking into the studio, I was introduced to Adam Scorgie, the producer of the excellent documentary about the marijuana industry in Canada *The Union: The Business Behind Getting High*. And immediately after this I had a chance to meet the one and only Pete McCormack, who was as ridiculously talented as an individual ever gets. Besides being the director of *I Am Bruce Lee* and several other films, Pete had written screenplays, published novels, and released several CDs of his own music. But other than establishing that he was a seriously gifted creative mind, listing all his accomplishments doesn't say much about the human being he was—and that's what struck me the most. My bullshit radar is often a curse, since within about ten seconds from shaking hands with someone I can already spot the least pleasant sides of their personality. Pete was something else. I got nothing but great vibes out of the man. By the time we sat down to chat about Bruce Lee, it was like talking to an old friend.

The whole conversation flowed effortlessly (well . . . the fact that the mic had been taped to my chest hair made it a little less effortless, but let's not get too picky). At one point, Pete's eyes lit up when I compared Bruce Lee to "a big middle finger raised toward any form of authority." He made me repeat that line a couple of times, just to make sure the sound was good, since he definitely wanted to include it in the finished documentary. Raised middle fingers were apparently becoming my trademark.

By the time I left, we were friends. I don't use the word "friend" often, but this was an exception. In the months and years to come, Pete and I would team up for a series of badass creative projects that I am ridiculously proud of. (Speaking of which, any TV exec among my readers is more than welcome to give us a call . . .)

By the time the documentary was released a few months later, Bruce's daughter, Shannon, had organized a premiere for the cast and crew. Getting to meet her was a real treat: you'd expect that during a night in honor of her father, when everyone wanted to talk to her, she'd be difficult to approach. But demonstrating zero ego and/or prima donna tendencies, Shannon came up to me to introduce herself and chat. She was very sweet and super easy to get along with.

Slightly different was my interaction with another guest. Some miscommunication almost led to my kicking some Iron Man's ass, or perhaps my getting knocked out by Robert Downey Jr., but all's well that ends well, so no superheroes had to be injured during the making of the *I Am Bruce Lee* premiere.

In any case, demonstrating that life is indeed weird and unpredictable, my *Godfather* impersonation during the trip to Wales led to the most glorious sixty-two seconds in the history of moviemaking. Since I had promised I'd take a shot of tequila for each second of screen-time I'd have above fifty, it made for an eventful evening.

ISABELLA INTERLUDE 15

Yakuza Style

Isabella at four years old.

Iz was telling me about her day at school. The conversation got interesting when she said, "Rowan is going to give me her ear for my birthday."

"You mean she is going to give you her earrings."

"No . . . her ear."

"Why, pray tell, does Rowan have to go Van Gogh for your birthday?"

"She broke a promise to me, so I told her to chop off her ear."

"And how did she respond?"

"She knows she broke the promise, so she said ok. She'll cut off her ear, put it in a box, and bring it to my birthday."

#YakuzaStyle

CHAPTER 50

PTSD

Almost a year to the day from when Elizabeth's symptoms had become severe enough as to require her first hospital trip, I ended up in the same hospital. And I took the same exact tests she took. And I lay on the very same MRI machine. If this was the universe showing a sense of humor, it failed to amuse me.

A couple of weeks earlier, I was in the gym hitting the weights and running. Nothing unusual there—no warning that serious problems were on the horizon. But my well-deserved sleep was interrupted only a few hours into it by the most intense muscular pain I had ever felt. It felt like a severe cramp—except for the fact that cramps last a few seconds and go away, while this still had me limping around hours later. Even though the edge of the pain eventually dulled, it never really went away.

No big deal, I thought. *I must have pushed too hard in the gym. I'll give it some rest and I'll be like new in a few days.*

A few days came and went, and the pain didn't decrease. On the contrary, it spread from my lower back all the way to my foot. And just to dispel any illusions that things would get solved on their own, the pain eventually expanded to my other leg as well.

By that point, I was officially freaked out. Seventeen thousand medical exams later, my doctor told me I had a crazy high level of inflammation in my body, which basically meant there was something quite wrong with me.

No shit.

Unfortunately, the results were not specific enough to point in any particular direction. Consultations with about a dozen different specialists didn't bring any solid diagnosis. "Yours is a very interesting case" was the comment I kept hearing from most of them—which I took as their way of saying, "You are sick, but we have no fucking clue how, or why, or what to do about it."

In the meantime, my symptoms kept getting worse. I was having a difficult time walking over long distances. The pain in my legs was such that picking up Isabella was a challenge. And just because things were so rosy already, I started developing some unexplained, persistent, low-grade fevers that would hang around for weeks. My doctors would offer worried, puzzled looks but nothing close to a diagnosis.

This was like the flashback from hell. It felt as if I was reliving what Elizabeth had gone through: the same sense of powerlessness, of dealing with increasingly worsening mysterious symptoms, and of not finding any answers. The possibility of death knocked on the door of my consciousness. This was all too eerily similar to the process that had led to Elizabeth's death. The thing that terrified me the most was the thought of leaving Isabella. That possibility gnawed at my soul and tortured my mind.

After three months of this, a friend suggested I check out a Chinese doctor who had worked miracles for her. I wasn't all that hopeful about it, but what did I have to lose by now?

Adding one more name to the list of doctors who couldn't help me wouldn't hurt. The dude looked a little like Yoda, and his place . . . well, it looked like a bomb had gone off in there. To make matters worse, I think he had studied his acupuncture techniques from torture manuals, because it was the most painful thing ever. But he seemed convinced that at least part of my problems had to do with a messed-up back, and that he could fix me (or at least that's what I understood in the funky brand of English that both he and I spoke). And sure enough, he did!

Sort of . . . the pain in my legs disappeared after a few treatments and the fevers were gone. I was ready to build the diminutive Chinese man a statue and kiss his feet every day of my life but, as amazing as his intervention had been, it had not addressed the root causes.

As a renewed bout of a second mystery illness a year later would demonstrate, my problems were not fully solved. This second bout was apparently unrelated to the one I had already had: the symptoms and everything else about it were different. The origin of the trouble was probably in my mind. Not that my physical symptoms weren't real. Hell . . . they were much more real than I wanted them to be. Over time, I developed digestive problems, crazy debilitating fatigue, and a myriad of all too real injuries. But at the roots of it all were my emotions.

Reading Dr. John Sarno's *The Divided Mind*—a master text about the psychosomatic origin of many diseases—was almost freaky. I felt like Sarno had been peeking over my shoulder and observing me before writing down those pages. In them, I found a blow-by-blow description of everything going on with me, and a flawless explanation of what caused it.

As much as I had been able to push through everything that had happened and soldier on, my personality was scarred by some serious PTSD. I had managed to keep my attitude in check, and never gave in to the feelings of desperation that were trying to run me down. This had allowed me to remain strong on the outside, facing everything that life had been throwing my way. But my body had paid a price nonetheless. The physical symptoms were the last link in a chain of anger. Anger that Elizabeth was dead. Anger that I had not brought her lasting happiness, despite trying with all my strength. Anger at losing my house. Anger at the academic motherfuckers who shut their doors in my face precisely at a time when I needed help the most. Anger that life's obligations didn't allow me to sleep as much as I needed or take a break from it all. Anger for all the times when I felt I was a shitty parent. Anger for the pressure that I always put on myself. Anger for the times when I'd fall short of my expectations. Anger that any moment of joy I experienced was regularly marred by a sense of guilt over the fact that I was still alive while Elizabeth was not. Anger for every person I knew and loved who had been served a dose of pain and tragedy. Anger toward death, sickness, and old age. Anger over this damn sense of vulnerability that never left me. Anger at the sense of absolute powerlessness that trapped me. Anger at the unfairness of the universe . . .

Yeah . . . the more I thought about it, the more I had to take into account that there was a teeny tiny chance that I had some anger issues. I clearly hadn't fully dealt with some dark emotions boiling under the surface, and yet I wasn't entirely sure how to deal with them more than I had already. This remains an open question to this day.

ISABELLA INTERLUDE 16

The Hobbit

Isabella at five years old.

Iz: "I want to see the movie . . ."

Not the most helpful hint I have ever received.

Me: "Which movie?"

Iz: "The one where they cut his grandfather's head off and he wants revenge."

Me: "You'll have to be a little more specific than that. Half of my movies include someone's head getting chopped off and someone getting revenge."

After further questioning, I found out that Iz wanted to watch *The Hobbit*. Not only did she end up sitting through all three hours of the extended version of the film, but she didn't get scared. And the following day, she asked to watch it again.

Parental pride!

CHAPTER 51

The Podfather

While I was still in the clutches of mystery illness #1, I received a call that was going to have a huge impact on my life.

My book *50 Things You're Not Supposed to Know: Religion*, was due to be released soon. My publisher, Disinformation, had hired a gentleman named Matt Staggs to promote it. And Matt had apparently started working his magic. On this particular day, Matt called to let me know that the gods had smiled upon us and doors had miraculously opened: I was scheduled to appear on the Joe Rogan Experience and The Adam Carolla Show, two of the most popular podcasts in the world. Matt was elated—trying to get me on those shows had been a Hail Mary on his part, but somehow both of them had said yes.

As much as I appreciated his efforts, I wasn't exactly in the mood to share in his enthusiasm. I had been lying in bed for a week, with unexplained fevers sapping my energy and crazy powerful muscle pains in my legs. Just trying to have breakfast sitting at a table seemed like a challenge. My mind was more concerned with whether I'd be alive in another month than with career opportunities.

Two of the biggest podcasts in the world? Forgive me if I fail to give a fuck.

Not having the energy to think about it too much was actually a good thing. It prevented me from psyching myself out. There's something a bit humbling about sitting down for a one-on-one conversation that will be downloaded and listened to by half a million people. Focusing on that too much can make one self-conscious and inhibit spontaneity. Luckily, or unluckily, I wasn't in a position to do that. My damn mystery fever was still with me by the time I parked my car outside of Joe's studio.

Joe was one of those few, rare animals who had carved out a career for themselves doing exactly what they wanted. In Joe's case, this meant doing many different things: in addition to his full-time job as commentator for UFC, he had another full-time gig as a comedian, had been the host of the TV show *Fear Factor*, and was running one of the world's most successful podcasts. On top of this, he still found the time to work out religiously and be a father. The man had clearly mastered the secret of fitting eighty hours into a twenty-four-hour day, or perhaps he had cloned himself—I'm not sure. In either case, what he was doing didn't seem humanly possible. He truly lived many lives rolled into one.

Part of the reason for the success of his podcast laid precisely in his ability to be multiple things at once. This permitted him to appeal to different audiences simultaneously. The rough-around-the-edges, combat-sports-loving crowd dug the fact that Joe was the prototype of the alpha male who had fought as a professional kickboxer, had a black belt in Brazilian jiu jitsu, was adored by women, and able to lift crazy weights. Comedy fans knew him as a stand-up god who had the audience rolling with laughter with the grossest jokes one minute, only to drop some enlightening concept the next . . . And that's the thing that some people forgot about Joe: he wasn't simply a really tough and really funny guy—he was also incredibly smart. On the podcasts, he regularly had guests from the most different fields, and somehow always managed to speak their language. He could talk intelligently for hours about anything—from sports to politics, from religion to science.

One of the things that stood out in my mind was how Joe had been able to convince some very macho types that it was cool to develop other sides as well. Many of them would have immediately been turned off hearing someone talk about nerdy and/or more spiritual subjects, but they were willing to listen to Joe, since no one would dispute his credentials as a bona fide badass: "If Joe is into these things, maybe I can be into them too without people thinking I'm gay."

Joe, for example, was a fierce advocate for the spiritual benefits of psychedelics. People with shaved heads and covered in tattoos who spend their free time training in combat sports are not exactly the natural bedfellows of hippies raving about psychedelic substances, but somehow Joe could bring these different crowds together and inspire them to be more complex and nuanced than they would have been otherwise.

Speaking of mind-altering substances, Joe confirmed all the rumors when he offered me a joint within about thirty seconds of shaking hands with me and introducing himself. (For the legally minded among you, he clearly only did so after ascertaining that I was the legitimate owner of a current medical marijuana card . . . You know . . . we wouldn't wanna break the law, clearly.)

It was obvious that Joe didn't know what to make of me. He had heard I was a professor in college and it seemed like he expected somebody formal and serious. The more we talked, the more he began getting a read on me, and the easier the conversation became. The high-quality sativa we had smoked cleared my mind and made me forget about the fever. Chatting with Joe was lots of fun.

The whole experience was completely different from being on The Adam Carolla Show. On Joe's podcast, the guest was 50 percent of the equation, engaging Joe in a back-and-forth conversation for one, two, or even three hours of nonstop verbal ping pong. And talking with Joe was like riding a bull on speed: you never knew where the conversation would turn next. The only guarantee was the intensity of the pace. Adam was also hilarious and brilliant, but guests on his show were little more than props. Adam *was* the show from beginning to end. The job of the guest was to offer Adam ideas and stimuli that he could use as assists, enabling him to slam-dunk another great joke. The whole thing was radically unlike being on Joe's podcast.

This was to be only my first of many repeat visits to record with Joe. By the time we were done with the episode, Joe and I had hit it off well, but I still didn't fully grasp what a turning moment this would be for me. I archived it under the "fun experiences" file, and that was it. The first wake-up call came with the volume of emails and Facebook messages I received over the following week. I spent about five to six hours a day replying to Joe's listeners. It was super encouraging to know that there were so many people out there enjoying what we brought to the table. By inviting me on the show, Joe had gently allowed me to bypass traditional forms of media and connect directly with thousands of like-minded people spread all over the world.

The days of having to depend on book reviews and other types of corporate-vetted media were over. Before being on Joe's podcast, I knew next to nothing about the podcasting world: I was told it was kind of like radio but I was free to cuss at will—which was good enough for me. Eventually, I'd realize that podcasting cut off the bureaucratic middlemen who stood between content creators and audiences. It wasn't simply a new type of media. It was a much better type of media. And Joe was its number one evangelist. Almost anyone I'd end up knowing in the podcasting world was connected with Joe in one way or another. From Duncan Trussell to Chris Ryan, from Aubrey Marcus to Amber Lyon, from Dan Carlin to Tait Fletcher—and many, many more—all of us either started our podcasts directly due to Joe's encouragement, or greatly benefited from being on his show. The seeds to my own podcast were planted on the Joe Rogan Experience. He was truly the godfather of podcasting.

ISABELLA INTERLUDE 17

Kids and Nightmares

Isabella at five years old.

Iz fell asleep and within two minutes she woke up very agitated. I was still right next to her, so she saw me, calmed down a bit, and asked, "Why do little kids have so many nightmares?"

I had never really thought about it, but I offered this as a reply, "It's because you don't control anything. All day long, big people tell you what to do, when to do it, and how to do it. You have very little choice about anything happening in your life. You are too little to take care of yourself, so people are constantly arranging your life for you without you having much of a say in this. But as you grow up, you gain a bit more choice over how you live your life, so some of that anxiety goes away, and you have fewer nightmares."

Thoughtful pause for about five seconds as she considered my words.

And then she started laughing her ass off.

"What's so funny?" I asked.

Iz: "After you explained it to me, it's not that scary anymore. It's a little scary, but not much. It's more funny than scary."

Me: "Glad I could help. Good night."

Iz: "Good night."

And with that, she passed out for twelve hours.

CHAPTER 52

How I Met Duncan Trussell and How a Drink Served in a London Bar Ended Up Being Named after Us

"You have to meet Duncan Trussell and record a podcast with him. He's a genius. I'm sure you guys would have an amazing conversation. You owe it to the world, man. People would go crazy over it."

The epic Matt Staggs was back. Considering how well things had worked out with Joe (Rogan) and Adam (Carolla), I felt duty-bound to trust him. I had vaguely heard of Duncan as a comedian who had been on Joe's podcast a bunch of times, but didn't know much about him beyond that. So, I did what all worshippers of the gods of the Internet do in this kind of situation. In humble supplication, I directed my query to the oracle of Google to see what the gods had to say about Mr. Trussell.

The gods at times are playful pranksters, or perhaps I was just in an uncharitable moment, but the first YouTube clip that I found of Duncan failed to excite me.

Matt, I thought, *I know you see something in this guy, but I don't get it. From what I see, he seems like a deranged dumbass...*

How little I knew...

Right now, almost three years later, I am typing these words at Gate 24, Terminal 2, at LAX, where I am about to board a plane headed for Vancouver to record a podcast with Duncan in front of a live audience. In the last few years, I've recorded probably a dozen podcasts with him—each one more fun than the next. More importantly, I consider Duncan a friend and a great human being.

In any case, back to nearly three years ago.

By the time I parked my car, walked up to Duncan's house, and saw him standing at the door, I immediately knew that Matt was right and that I was a judgmental asshole. The fact that Duncan was a hell of a person was clear before we even shook hands.

As it would become even more obvious in the course of the conversation, and in the many conversations that followed, Duncan was indeed as brilliant as advertised. He possessed an unparalleled ability to string words together in hilarious and at the same time philosophically profound fashion. His use of language had a Tom Robbins quality to it. It's a crime Duncan never turned to writing books. His verbal mastery is rare even among top-rated novelists.

Our podcast chat couldn't have gone better. Neither one of us had any idea where the conversation would take us, but somehow we kept flowing as if we had scripted the whole thing. It felt like musicians jamming in spontaneous yet flawless harmony. We mixed philosophy, spirituality, and our brand of proudly lowbrow humor while pulling no punches and baring our souls. Matt had called it right: Duncan was definitely a great verbal sparring partner for me. Luckily, Duncan, Matt, and I were not the only ones to think so. His listeners dug our interaction enough to request repeats time and time again.

One of these repeated visits to the Trussell lair, which also doubled as his recording studio, produced what is possibly my favorite podcasting moment of all time. Never one to shy away from intense conversations, in this particular episode Duncan weaved the dialogue in a very personal direction. I can't remember how we arrived there, but I ended up speaking about everything that had happened with Elizabeth, and what had followed her death. The deeper we delved, the more intimate, raw, and real it got.

And then we reached a point where words couldn't accompany us. We had said everything that could be said. I ended my story and there was really nothing left for me to add. This was where Duncan did something beautiful: he didn't try to rush to fill the silence that followed. He just sat there with me while the machine kept recording our non-conversation. Seconds went by. And then more of them. That long silence we shared before finally speaking again and wrapping up the episode remains to this day my favorite moment in podcasting.

In many ways, the genesis of this very book you are reading was born in that moment. The feedback that Duncan's listeners offered us about that conversation made it crystal clear that people benefited more whenever we touched on intensely personal experiences rather than simply speaking in more abstract philosophical terms. To put it simply, experiences lived on one's skin speak louder than philosophy. As Nietzsche wrote, in the opening quote at the beginning of this book, "Of all that is written, I love only what a person has written with his blood."

The highly touching emails I received from people about how listening to the story had helped them deal with issues in their own lives convinced me to write this book. If what I have been through can be of use to someone else, why not?

In addition to spawning this book, that particular episode with Duncan led to other, rather bizarre consequences. An artist named Paul Klawiter took the audio of a Zen story I told Duncan (about tigers and strawberries), animated it, and put it on YouTube. I was turned into origami by some creative listener. And a cocktail bar in London decided to name one of their drinks after a reference in the conversation. So, if you are ever in the UK and end up tasting something named "Strawberry Connection," please raise your glass to us.

ISABELLA INTERLUDE 18

Facing Fear with Pink Band-Aids

Isabella at five years old.

It all began when I sliced my finger with a knife. I've handled a million knives in my life and never cut myself, but I was too busy torturing myself thinking that I was a shitty parent to pay attention to the blade. I was so damn tired that I parked Iz in front of the TV for hours with minimal attention from me. I would have paid someone in gold just to avoid interacting with her—this at a time when she was sick and needed extra attention. I sucked . . . I know.

Hence, sense of guilt. Hence, sliced finger and blood spraying all around.

Iz saw my finger and began making whimpering sounds expressing a mix of fear, disgust, empathy for my pain, and more disgust by how gross all the blood looked to her. I knew I didn't cut any tendon or ligament or anything important. It was just a particularly bloody surface cut, so I mustered my most mellow, relaxed voice and said, "Iz, there's no reason to be afraid of blood. Look at me. I'm the one who is bleeding here, but do I look afraid to you?"

She stopped whimpering and shook her head.

"People freak out when they bleed, but often it's more of a mental thing than real pain. They make their own pain worse by thinking about how gross the blood is. The pain is a little bad. But their fear makes it really bad. It's silly. Blood is neither gross nor scary. But you and I are too tough to be scared of it, right?"

More nodding.

"Good. So, now you know you don't need to be scared of it, and you have just become tougher than most other kids."

She looked at the blood again, but was now completely calm.

So, I figured I would up the stakes a little. I opened up the cut a bit more to spray some blood out and make a game out of it. She usually hated disinfecting her own scrapes, so I had her pour alcohol on my cut. I acknowledged that alcohol hurt, but also that it was good for avoiding infection, and that ultimately the pain would go away.

After that she couldn't stop telling me how silly it was that most kids were scared of blood. But just to make sure everything would be ok, she insisted on putting on my finger a pink Band-Aid with princesses on it (Jasmine, Aurora, and Ariel—in case you are wondering).

And it is with the cooperation of my pink-decorated finger that I'm now typing this.

CHAPTER 53

The Drunken Taoist

Once upon a time, legions of middlemen stood between content creators and audiences. They were the puppet masters holding the strings of the creative world. No matter how talented they were, aspiring writers, radio hosts, musicians, journalists, filmmakers, teachers, etc., had little choice but to bow down and make sacrifices on the altars of the industry bosses who had the power to decide who would receive their blessings and who would be kicked to the curb.

And then the Internet came along, and everything changed.

If the Muses are whispering in your ears, if the great American novel is waiting to be midwifed into existence by your typing fingers, if the Resurrection of the Dead is what will happen when the no-longer-living will rise from their graves to dance to the beat of the song humming in your brain, then you can thank the gods that you are alive today. Never before in history has any human being had the opportunity to reach millions of other people without needing to kiss the asses of the entertainment mafia. YouTube, iTunes, Twitter, Facebook . . . these are the creator's best friends, allowing you to bypass the traditional systems of content distribution.

In that phase of my life, this turned out to be quite welcome news for me. It is no secret, in fact, that being on good terms with any type of establishment has never been one of my natural talents. I regularly have little but contempt for them and they—with equal regularity—hate my guts. Just twenty years ago, I would have been shit out of luck, but now a whole different game is possible.

Each time I appeared as a guest on a podcast was yet another lesson in the reality of this new world. The power of the medium to reach people from all walks of life, all over the world, never failed to astound me. Despite this, and despite receiving zillions of emails from listeners inviting me to take the plunge, I still didn't think of running my own podcast.

My spare time being nonexistent, I tried for a while to hide behind any possible excuse not to go for it. At one point, just to dissuade the people urging me on a daily basis to start recording, I told them I'd do it if I didn't have to worry about learning all the technical aspects of the field—in other words, if someone volunteered to take care of everything from editing to staging episodes. I was sure no one would step up and that this would be the end of it. Within about five minutes, a gentleman named Rich Evirs replied to the thread on Facebook saying he was a film editor with a studio available just a few miles from me. Minutes later, another gentleman named Evan Culver added that he could put up the website, stage episodes, and take care of all web-related issues. And my friend Jeff Hendricks also tossed his name into the hat to help out.

Oh damn . . . kiss goodbye to your excuses, Daniele.

I called the always-epic Duncan Trussell, recruited him as the first guest for the show, and episode one was on its way.

Anyone who didn't already know me or Duncan probably ended up running for their lives. Episode one would flow from deep philosophical discussions about the nature of the Tao to Duncan's gross tales about used fleshlights. Probably half of the people who clicked just to check it out quickly regretted their choice, but the other half came to love us. Before I fully understood what was going on, I had thousands of listeners from around the world—largely, no doubt, thanks to Duncan and Joe Rogan pushing some of their listeners my way.

Could any of this have ever happened just a few years earlier? Can you imagine how radio executives would have responded to the idea of *me* hosting a show?

"Does that guy even speak English? Screw him and his thick Italian accent. No one is going to listen. Calling the podcast *The Drunken Taoist*!? That's a sure way to scare away sponsors. And what the hell is the show about anyway? It's all over the place. One day he talks about sport and the next is philosophy. One day is religion and the next is sex. He needs to make up his mind. He needs to fit in a category—in a recognizable label. Maybe we can talk about it if he learns to speak English and stick to one topic. Until then, there's no market for this shit."

But thanks to the gods of the Internet, I could bypass these sorry motherfuckers and their silly rigidity, and reach straight for an audience that liked what I had to offer precisely because it was unlike what they could find through more conventional channels. The eclectic nature of the show was its strength, not its weakness. When I was asked what the podcast was about, I made it clear from the start that I cared for anything making life intense, passionate, and worth living. Whatever met this requirement was fine by me—regardless of which particular field it belonged to. *The Drunken Taoist* was about a temperature more than a topic.

The podcast gave me the gift of basking in the liberating feeling of not having to worry about upholding a certain image or fitting in a specific category. I could afford to be myself 100 percent—just radical honesty, with no fear of the consequences. If this wasn't already its own reward, even better was finding out that people responded to it. Very quickly, we attracted a sizeable international audience. And those sweet souls who are Chris Odell (from Datsusara), Aubrey Marcus (from Onnit), and Bennett Grunberg (from Sure Design T-Shirts) even volunteered to sponsor the podcast.

The flood of incoming emails wasn't simply gratifying, but also revealed something profound. Somewhere in Omaha, Guadalajara, Osaka, Königsberg, and a million other places, were individuals of uncommon sensitivity who felt utterly alienated by their surroundings. When they tried to share their ideas with the people around them, they got back blank stares and heads shaking. The difficulty in finding someone who related to their unconventional thinking made them feel weird and foreign in their own backyard, mushroom spores from outer space that had landed by chance in those lands. No roots and little connection to those around them. But the right podcasts broke the spell for them. They allowed them to tune in to conversations that made them realize there were like-minded individuals out there. This discovery was to many of them both exhilarating and inspiring. And each email telling me how listening to my podcast had pushed someone to change their lives in a radically happier direction gave me renewed energy to record more.

The diversity of our listeners amused me and humbled me. The conversations happening in our Culver City studio would reach places I had never dreamed of. People listened while biking through the streets of Copenhagen, chopping wood in the snow in Quebec, driving through the mountains of Western

India at midnight, hiding in a bathroom in Mexico as a drug war massacre was taking place outside their door, running a restaurant in Indonesia, cleaning office toilets during a night shift in the US, operating their own ecolodge in Malawi, tending to their marijuana gardens in Australia, or practicing archery in the UK. (In case you are wondering I didn't make up a single detail in this list.) Among our listeners were Israelis taking shelter in a bunker to avoid Hamas' rockets and Palestinians studying abroad and worrying for their family during an Israeli offensive. American soldiers on duty in Afghanistan and Iraq, NBA and NFL players, Australian aborigines, and full-blooded Cherokees all listened to our podcast.

And then, of course, there were the guests: plenty of amazing human beings I would probably never have crossed paths with had it not been for the podcast.

At a time when I was trying not to drown in an ocean of grief and heartbreak, the podcast gave me the energy to say, "Fuck pain. Fuck heartbreak. I'm still in love with life."

ISABELLA INTERLUDE 19

Cannibalism

Isabella at five years old.

Iz: "Humans are no good to eat. Once I tried eating my own arm and it was terrible."

CHAPTER 54

In the Beginning Was Fear

If this book had followed the linear course that literary agents love, the arc of this story would have taken me from being a scared wimp to transforming myself into the kind of man who knows neither fear nor doubts. A few pages before the end, I should have slayed the dragon, saved the day, and ridden off into the sunset.

Too bad that my life is not a Disney story, and I don't want to sell it as such. I am certainly less prone to be fear's slave than I used to be, but I still have my moments when insecurities clutch my soul, and I revert for a little while to being what I was. The times when I am able to silence all insecurities and KO fear, though, always coincide with being able to adopt a particular state of mind. Since you have been a most gracious reader, and I deeply appreciate your sticking with me to the end of this book, I'll try to capture it for you in as few words as possible.

Here we go.

In the beginning was fear—the fear that everything that has a body experiences once it realizes we live in a predatory universe, a universe in which absolutely everything gets to be eaten, if not by the sharp fangs of a predator, then by time itself. And Fear became our God. And it began to rule over our lives, shrink our willingness to dare, and rob us of the beauty of it all.

Fear is written in the deepest layer of our DNA. You can't run away from it. You can't escape it. It's so pervasive that plenty of people try to exorcise the demon. Religions, philosophies, advertisements, motivational speakers . . . They all tell you that if you make the jump and follow their cure, you'll no longer have anything to fear. They tell you that there are no monsters hiding under your bed. They promise you safety from everything you fear. They promise you a sense of empowerment. They promise you victory against all odds.

The reality is that they are trying to sell you something.

The monster is indeed under your bed, after all. The reality is that you have every good reason to be afraid, because everything you fear is on your tracks right now, and will eventually catch up to you and destroy everything you loved and everything you are.

Welcome to the world, motherfuckers.

So why *Not Afraid*? Wouldn't it be more appropriate to call this book *Scared Shitless and Rightfully So*?

Because being scared doesn't help you. Reality is uglier and harsher than anything we like to admit to ourselves, and yet it's pointless to be scared since your fear will not protect you. Fear is only useful if it alerts you of a danger you can avoid, but if there's no possible way to avoid it, if it's inevitable that it'll crush you no matter how hard you fight, then what's the point of being afraid? If you have no hope of survival, what's left to be afraid of?

The only thing you'll succeed in doing is spoiling this very second when the forces that will destroy you haven't stepped onto the stage yet.

Yes, you will not get out of here alive. But so what? All the more reason to celebrate right here and right now. Let's pop the champagne before all hell breaks loose. Squeeze every last ounce of orgasmic ecstasy from the present moment. And when the monster finally climbs out from under your bed, at least you'll have a good reason to smile before he devours you. You are already dead. Let's have a party in the meantime.

Acknowledgments

Infinite thanks to those humans who have brightened my life, including the following: Franco Bolelli, Gloria Mattioni, Isabella Han Bolelli, Savannah Em, Elizabeth Han, Mark Cheng, Ale Rossi, Aubrey Marcus, Whitney Miller, Bostjan Nachbar, Chris Odell, Bennett Grunberg, Pete McCormack, Mike Vallely, Cody Em, Robert Subiaga, Rich Evirs, Evan Culver, Dan Carlin, Rocco Attisani, Aronne Dell'Oro, Bruno Dorella, Marlon Mercado, Roberto Bonomelli and Lory, Zina, and Stelio Bolelli, Marina Mattioni, Liliana Germani, Duncan Trussell, Joe Rogan, Chris Ryan, Amber Lyon, Tait Fletcher, Sean Faust, Thaddeus Russell, Jeff Hendricks, Chris Stiles, Sif Goodale, Manuela Mantegazza, Liezel Legaspi, Kriszanne Napalan, Ernestine Segura, Matt Staggs, Tatianna Em, Christian Reid, Tania Reid, Chad Morrison, Viva Rankel, Harut Tarakhchyan, Emanuel Carnevale, Shannon Lee, Federico Giordano, Julio Perez, Rick Tucci, Mary Jo Colli and Ilaria, Gary Baddeley, Jan Johnson, Mark Adachi, AJ Hawk, Giancarlo Serafino, Sarah Majocchi, Tom and Alexa Robbins, Amy and Wes Tang, Roberto Banchini and his tribe, James Weddell, Cicily Tiger-Weddell, Atticus Hawk Zephier, John Evans, Will Ford, Jane Dabel, Shawn Brennan, John Torres, Li Schroeder, Rachel Pugh, Giorgio Presca and Erika Pozzobon, Shannon Seta,

Daniel Guedea, Jack Clark, Litty Mathew and Melkon Khosrovian, Emily and Jamie Ludovise, Michelle Panameno, Annie and Mike and Michaela Esposito, Troy Johnson, Tim Cartmell, Dennis Jelinek, Sharon Wikel, Kendall Blair, Al Herrera, Steve Chan, Kolja Fuchs, Leo Hirai, Alessandra Chiricosta, Roberto Tofani and Iris, Alan Predolin, Eugene and Margaret Carpenter, Sam Sheridan, Sumati Bonsai, Bryan Kest, José Camacho, Junella Chin, Graham Hancock, Paul Scarlata and Elisa Chun, Marcus Trumpp, Nic Gregoriades, Andrea Zingoni, Albert and Tina Ohanian, Teodoro Armenteros, Arthur and Janelle and Tasman Rosenfeld, Kyla Mares, Jun Lee, Marco Mandrino, Federico Rossi, and Chimie Moxham.

About the Author

Photo by Savannah Em

Daniele Bolelli, MA, is a writer, college professor, and martial artist. He is the author of several books, including *On the Warrior's Path* and *Create Your Own Religion*. He is the host of *The Drunken Taoist* podcast.

Visit him online at:

www.danielebolelli.com

https://twitter.com/DBolelli

www.facebook.com/pages/Daniele-Bolelli/437645359708174